THE MODERN MYSTIC

A PRACTICAL GUIDE TO MAGIC, MYSTICISM, AND ECLECTIC SPIRITUALITY

THOMAS PETERS

First Edition

Paperback ISBN: 979-8-9992428-0-8
Hardcover ISBN: 979-8-9992428-3-9
EBook ISBN: 979-8-9992428-1-5

TABLE OF CONTENTS

Section I: Foundations of Spirituality

Section II: Foundations of Magic

Section III: Advanced Magic

Section IV: Folk Traditions

SECTION I:

FOUNDATIONS OF SPIRITUALITY

"We are not human beings having a spiritual experience.
We are spiritual beings having a human experience."

— Pierre Teilhard de Chardin

1

INTRODUCTION

Western society stands at the brink of a new religious renaissance, one that challenges the authority of organized religion and embraces a more personal, eclectic approach to spirituality. Modern revivals of ancient practices like witchcraft and paganism are gaining followers at an unprecedented rate, with some estimates suggesting these communities are doubling in size every 18 months. Spiritual traditions that were once dismissed as primitive or suppressed as heretical are now being re-examined as powerful tools for personal transformation and connection. For many, this shift represents a desire to reconnect with ancestral wisdom, to honor nature, and to rediscover meaning through direct experience rather than external authority. In choosing this path, people are not abandoning spirituality, but actively reclaiming it!

If you are reading this book, you likely have felt a pull towards exploring your spiritual side. Maybe you sense a deeper purpose in life, but that calling eludes clear definition? Or perhaps you are interested in learning more about magic, but don't know where to start? While the internet is an incredibly rich database of knowledge for spirituality, it can be equally overwhelming to sift through the sheer onslaught of information that is available.

Throughout this book, I aim to guide you through a focused yet flexible exploration of magic and spirituality, helping you discover a path that aligns with your personal beliefs, goals, and values. We will begin by establishing a foundation of spiritual knowledge, with concepts like energy, magic, and animism. These serve as the building blocks for many spiritual practices, offering a shared language for understanding how certain unseen forces have shaped human experience. From there, we will travel through time to explore pagan and monotheistic religious systems as they existed throughout both the ancient and medieval world. With this foundation set, we will ultimately cover a wide range of magical practices, from nature-based witchcraft, to ceremonial magic, and even folk traditions. Each chapter is meant to help deepen your understanding of the spiritual world, while also providing useful information to draw from in your own practice. While the chapters follow a very purposeful order, you are welcome to skip around to the topics that resonate with you most!

Before getting ahead of ourselves, let's first establish what spirituality actually is and what role it plays in established religious systems. Spirituality is often thought to be vague or abstract, but its definition is surprisingly clear: "the quality of being concerned with the human spirit or soul as opposed to material or physical things." Put simply, it's the deliberate exploration of what lies beyond the five senses. For some, spirituality begins and ends with a belief in a higher power. For others, it evolves into a lifelong pursuit: a devotion to understanding the self, the sacred, and the intricate spaces in between. Both are genuine expressions of spirituality, differing only in intensity, not in authenticity.

Religion, by contrast, is the structured system of beliefs, rituals, and practices that someone might follow in *pursuit* of spirituality. They often use stories and symbols to help humans connect to their divine purpose, which is also why they are so effective at bringing communities together. Just as the cross reminds Christians of Christ's sacrifice for humanity, the Wiccan pentacle symbolizes the harmony of the five elements and provides a spiritual anchor for many witches. Both serve as grounding symbols, helping practitioners understand their place in the universe and their connection to something greater than themselves.

While religion offers guidance and structure, it can sometimes feel restrictive, as it often prescribes specific rules for understanding the universe and your role within it. When it comes to spirituality, however, there are no "wrong" answers because you are simply exploring what feels right for you. You may choose to follow an existing religious path, blend several, or craft your own! Your spiritual journey is uniquely yours, and it may shift over time as your insights and needs evolve. Embrace the freedom to explore and to change, as each step you take will likely strengthen the values that matter most to you.

Above all, let this book be an invitation to question, experiment, and awaken the innate wisdom that already lives within you. Whether you're here to deepen an existing practice or to take your very first steps into the unknown, know that your curiosity is sacred. Let this be a space of exploration without judgment, where every path you take adds to your own spiritual identity. Trust that each experience will guide you to where you need to be and who you will ultimately become.

2

ENERGY

In magical and spiritual practice, energy is the medium of transformation. Practitioners learn to sense it, raise it, direct it, and release it. It moves through the body, through objects, through sacred space, and through intention. When people speak of feeling a certain "vibe," they are often describing a subtle awareness of energy. Some believe it can be transmitted through touch or sound, while others experience it in meditation, ritual, or even deep emotional connection. In this way, energy becomes the invisible language of the soul. It is not confined to one religion or culture. It is universal, experienced by mystics and healers throughout time. But it is also a topic that intersects with science, offering a bridge between ancient spiritual wisdom and modern understandings of our universe.

In physics, energy is defined as the capacity to do work. It takes many forms: heat, light, motion, electricity, magnetism. These energies shape the physical world and operate according to precise laws. Even solid objects are made of atoms, and those atoms are composed of vibrating particles. On the smallest level, what we think of as matter is actually energy in motion. Einstein's famous equation, $E = mc^2$, showed that matter and energy are not separate things. Matter is energy that has taken form. Everything in existence, from galaxies to human bodies, is a manifestation of energy condensed into patterns. This idea echoes many ancient beliefs that all things are born from a single, unified force.

In fact, some physicists have proposed that the fundamental building blocks of reality are not particles at all, but tiny vibrating strings of energy. This is the basis of string theory, a model in which all matter and forces arise from the different ways these strings vibrate. The idea is still theoretical, but it offers a vision of the universe that is deeply harmonious. It suggests that everything exists as vibration, frequency, and resonance. To mystics, this sounds very familiar. Many spiritual traditions have long described the universe as a song, a sound, or a sacred tone. If everything exists as a vibration of energy, then it no longer seems absurd to think that our thoughts, actions, and relationships may deeply impact the world around us. Suddenly, magic becomes very real.

The connection between energy and consciousness is also worth considering. In quantum physics, particles appear to exist in multiple states until they are observed. The act of observation seems to affect the outcome of real-life experiments. One of the best examples of this is the Double Slit Experiment, which baffled scientists in 1927 by proving that photons of light change their state between a particle and a wave based on whether or not an observer is present. That's right, it would seem as if the universe itself may somehow be aware of our existence, changing the state of light just by experiencing it! This has led some to suggest that consciousness may play a role in shaping reality. While this idea is still highly debated in science, it aligns closely with spiritual teachings that speak of intention and manifestation as a very real force of creation.

On the human level, energy is often described in terms of subtle anatomy. The body is not just a physical structure, but also an energetic one. Thus, many spiritual systems use breathwork, sound, and visualization in an attempt to shift and balance these energies. Even ritual and prayer rely on the idea that focused intention can move energy into alignment with a desired outcome, even if that outcome is simply the deepening of your relationship to a deity. Many believe that thoughts, emotions, and words carry energy that can affect both the self and the world. While understanding energy from a theoretical perspective is important, it is most often something that has to be *experienced* to be fully understood.

Energy is not something outside of you. It is your nature. You are both the source and the vessel of the universe's most powerful forces. Every action you take, every intention you hold, radiates energy into the world. Just as a pebble creates ripples in water, your energy creates ripples in the universe, creating real tangible change in your life and others. You do not need to become a physicist or a mystic to work with energy. You only need to pay attention. Energy speaks in feelings, sensations, and intuition. It is the thread that connects the seen and the unseen. The more you align with it, the more you become a conscious participant in the unfolding of your own life.

3

MAGIC

M agic is one of the most misunderstood aspects of spirituality. For many, the word conjures images of fantasy novels or cinematic illusions, but magic has existed as a deeply rooted part of human culture for thousands of years. It is not confined to fiction or superstition. It is the intentional act of working with unseen forces to influence reality. If energy is the medium of transformation, then think of magic as the language through which humans shape energy into an intended outcome. This may sound dramatic, but in practice, magic can be both subtle and profound. It may be as quiet as lighting a candle with purpose or as ceremonial as a full moon ritual under the stars.

Magic is, at its core, a language of intentional transformation. It is how spiritual practitioners focus their intention and direct energy toward a meaningful goal. Unlike religion, which often relies on a structured relationship with a deity, magic is more personal and experiential. It allows individuals to take an active role in shaping their reality, not through domination or control, but through alignment with natural and spiritual forces. In this way, magic becomes a dialogue between the unseen world within and the unfolding world around us.

Though magic and religion differ in structure and purpose, they often intersect in practice. Even traditions that explicitly condemn the use of magic frequently engage in rituals that operate through similar principles. Catholic blessings with holy water, the recitation of hymns, the burning of incense, the lighting of candles, and the act of prayer all involve setting intention and seeking connection with unseen forces. In Judaism, the chanting of sacred texts and the use of ritual objects are similarly magical in practice. In Islam, verses from the Quran are frequently recited for healing or protection, with the belief that divine power can be accessed and directed through intentional speech. Even in Christianity, a baptism establishes ritual covenant and symbolizes transformation of identity and soul. These are not just symbolic acts, they are spiritual technologies meant to shift energy, influence outcomes, and open channels to the divine.

The difference is often one of language and perception. What one tradition calls prayer, another calls spellwork. What one calls a miracle, another calls manifestation. The mechanics may vary, but the spiritual impulse remains the same. People desire to create change in their lives, to feel empowered, and to experience connection with something greater than themselves. Magic, in all its forms, seeks to meet that desire.

Of course, not every spiritual path includes magic as a central component. Some traditions focus more on inner transformation than external change. In Confucianism, the emphasis is on cultivating virtue, harmony, and moral integrity rather than on invoking supernatural forces. In many forms of Buddhism, the focus lies in meditation, mindfulness, and detachment from craving. These paths still seek profound transformation, but they do so through the refinement of thought, behavior, and perception rather than through rituals or symbols.

Yet even in these traditions, elements of magical thinking are present. Tibetan Buddhism, for example, incorporates intricate rituals, mantras, and visualizations that are intended to transform both the self and the world. In the mystical branches of Islam and Judaism (Sufism and Kabbalah) we find practices aimed at achieving union with the divine through symbolic language, numerology, and meditative exercises. These systems of magic were likely developed alongside their religions to help believers and skeptics move closer to their spiritual goals.

To practice magic is not to deny science or reason. It is to work with aspects of reality that are not always visible, but that are felt and experienced. When you light a candle and speak your intention into the flame, you are participating in a ritual that channels energy and meaning. When you craft a charm, write a sigil, or perform a ceremony under the full moon, you are weaving intention into the fabric of the world. These acts are not about fantasy. They are about focus, clarity, and sacred engagement with the present moment.

Magic does not require elaborate tools or rare ingredients. It requires presence. It requires belief in your own capacity to influence your life and a willingness to participate in the mystery of existence. Some people work with deities, spirits, or ancestors. Others focus purely on energy, symbols, or the power of the spoken word. Some follow strict traditions. Others create their own systems based on intuition and experience. All are valid.

There is no single way to do magic. What matters is the intention behind your actions and the alignment of your heart with your purpose. Magic can be used to heal, to protect, to inspire, to release, and to celebrate. It can help you mark the turning points of your life, grieve your losses, or call forth your dreams. It can be as gentle as a whispered blessing or as potent as a ritual that changes your understanding of yourself forever.

It is important to remember that magic is not a guarantee. It is not a way to control the world or bypass natural consequences. Rather, it is a way to engage more deeply with life, to recognize the sacred in everyday moments, and to move with purpose through a world that is constantly shifting. Like any practice, it requires respect, discernment, and care. Magic is a gift, not a shortcut.

Some people will go their entire lives without ever casting a spell or performing a ritual. That does not make their spirituality any less valid. Magic is not required for a meaningful spiritual life. But for those who feel drawn to it, it can become a source of empowerment and renewal. It can help you remember your own agency, your creativity, and your connection to the universe.

You do not have to master magic to benefit from it. You simply have to be willing to explore. Whether you are lighting a candle, speaking a word, or walking barefoot under the stars, your magic is already unfolding. It is not something you need to earn or acquire. It is already within you, waiting for you to recognize it.

As you move forward in this book, you will encounter many different systems of magical practice. Some are rooted in ancient traditions, while others are more modern and eclectic. All of them offer unique tools for working with energy, intention, and spirit. Use what resonates and leave what does not. Let your magic be a reflection of who you are and the values you hold.

4

ANIMISM

Having explored how energy moves through our bodies, intentions, and the fabric of reality itself, we now turn to one of the oldest spiritual understandings of this truth: animism. Let us travel back to the dawn of mankind, where we will explore the earliest expressions of human belief, upon which the roots of modern religion first began to form. Long before named gods or organized religion, before written scripture or temples, there was animism. It is the most ancient and widespread form of spiritual belief, one that views the entire world as alive with energy. In animism, everything is thought to carry spirit. The trees, the rivers, the rocks, the clouds, and even places and objects made by human hands, are all seen as having their own form of consciousness or spiritual essence.

At its core, animism is the understanding that the physical world and the spiritual world are not separate. They exist together, woven into the same fabric. When the wind stirs, it is not just a movement of air, but a presence. When you speak to a plant or sit with a stream, you are not simply imagining connection, but participating in a relationship. For animists, nature is not a backdrop. It is a nonstop conversation with the world itself.

This way of seeing the world is not limited to any one culture. It has been the foundation of indigenous spiritual systems on every continent. In Africa, Asia, the Americas, the Pacific Islands, and Northern Europe, animism has formed the basis of how communities understood their place in the world, and is thought to originate from as far back as the Paleolithic Period. These traditions often did not think of animism as a religion or belief. It was simply reality. It was how you treated the land, how you listened to the animals, and how you survived changing climates.

One of the most important values in animist traditions is reciprocity. It is the idea that all good relationships must be mutual. If you take from the earth, you must give something back. If you harvest a plant, you offer thanks. If you cross a river, you ask for safe passage. These are not just acts of politeness, they are sacred agreements that maintain harmony between humans and nature. Animism teaches that you are part of a living world that is always watching and responding. In this sense, animism is not about worshipping nature, but living in cooperation with it. The deer, the mountain, the storm, the fire—none of these are gods in the traditional sense, but all are treated with the respect given to spiritual beings. This respect shows up in stories, songs, offerings, and rituals that help humans remember their responsibilities to the greater whole.

Modern society has largely lost this connection. In the name of progress, we have learned to label and measure nearly all aspects of the world in pursuit of resource extraction. We have treated the earth as something separate from us, as a "Giving Tree" to be used and abused rather than a living system to be honored. In this context, animism becomes more than just a spiritual perspective. It becomes a reminder of what we once knew. It becomes a way to heal the growing sense of isolation and disconnection that so many people feel today.

In magical practice, animism provides a powerful foundation. When a practitioner calls upon the elements or offers something to a spirit, they are acting from the belief that the world is alive and aware.

Magic becomes a dialogue rather than a demand. You are not forcing your will onto nature. You are working with it, building relationships with the forces around you. This is why so many magical paths include rituals invoking the elements of earth, air, fire, and water. These are not just symbols. They are presences with which you can physically interact with in the natural world.

You do not need to belong to any specific tradition to practice animism. What you need is awareness. The ability to slow down, to observe, and to listen. The spirit of a place will not always speak in words. It may show itself through a feeling, a sudden change in weather, a repeated animal encounter, or an intuitive knowing that rises within you. Over time, you begin to recognize the patterns. You begin to sense when a place welcomes you and when it does not.

Many animist cultures also hold deep relationships with their ancestors. Ancestors are seen not only as family members who have passed on, but as continuing presences in the world. They may offer guidance, protection, or simply remind you of where you came from. In many traditions, the line between ancestor and spirit is thin. When you speak to your grandmother in prayer, or light a candle for those who came before you, you are practicing a form of animism. You are acknowledging that death is not an ending, but a change in relationship.

In daily life, animism can be practiced in small but powerful ways. You might speak out loud to the plants as you water them. You might offer a few crumbs to the birds in the morning. You might pause before stepping onto a trail and ask the forest for permission. These actions may seem simple, but they carry a quiet weight. They create a habit of reverence and remind you that you are part of something greater than yourself.

Animism is not a belief that demands obedience. It does not ask you to memorize laws or recite dogma. It asks only that you pay attention and treat the world around you as something sacred. As you move forward in your spiritual journey, animism can serve as a foundation for just about any form of magic. It brings depth and respect to every ritual you perform. It brings meaning to the tools you use, the spaces you enter, and the energies you work with. Most importantly, it helps you reconnect. Not just with spirit, but with the world that spirit lives in.

5

PAGANISM

As animistic tribes began to develop into more advanced agricultural societies, paganism emerged as a more structured system of honoring the divine through mythology, ritual, and the worship of many gods. Historically, paganism has referred to any set of spiritual beliefs and practices that are distinct from the major Abrahamic religions (Christianity, Islam, and Judaism). While this is still true, paganism is more accurately characterized today as any form of polytheistic animism. To put it simply, paganism is nature-based worship that includes a pantheon of multiple gods, each holding their own domain over nature. It is an attempt by early humans to connect with and understand nature by animating its various aspects into human-like gods, which are far easier to relate to and form a relationship with.

Some of the earliest recorded evidence of pagan worship dates back as far as 35,000 BC, with the use of carved figurines in the form of an exaggerated female body. Known as the "Venus Figurines", these idols are thought to have had some ritual significance, perhaps for fertility. Since then, archaeologists have uncovered hundreds of pagan idols depicting everything from animals to human body parts. Often these idols were made out of malleable materials like clay, stone, bone, or ivory for their ability to be carved into various shapes. Early humans may have used, for instance, a stone idol in the shape of a deer to ensure a successful hunt for their tribe. This form of worship would ultimately become the basis behind much larger and more established forms of paganism, which we see in cultures like ancient Greece, Rome, Egypt, and Scandinavia.

Paganism flourished throughout the ancient world and was directly responsible for some of the most incredible monuments ever built in human history. Stonehenge, The Parthenon, The Pyramids, The Colossus of Rhodes—each are thought to have had some sort of pagan influence in their construction. It wasn't until the late Roman Empire that the world began to see a major decline in paganism, with widespread persecution at the hands of Christians, Jews, and eventually Muslims. Especially in Europe during the fourth and early fifth centuries, harsh Christian legislation made it practically impossible for people to continue their ancestral pagan worship without being tortured, killed, or exiled from society. Pagan temples were destroyed to be replaced with Christian churches, and many pagan holidays were replaced with Christian ones (often held on the exact same days) to aid in the transition over to the Abrahamic system of faith.

This pattern of religious suppression wasn't limited to the rise of Christianity. In the 7th century, the rapid expansion of Islam also led to widespread persecution of pagan communities, particularly across the Arabian Peninsula and North Africa. The Quran explicitly condemned idolatry, and early Islamic leaders viewed pagan practices as incompatible with monotheism. As a result, many pre-Islamic traditions, deities, and sacred sites were systematically erased or absorbed into the new religious framework. In Mecca, for example, the Kaaba (once a sanctuary housing numerous tribal idols) was stripped of its polytheistic associations and re-sanctified as a monotheistic site devoted solely to Allah. Pagan tribes that resisted conversion were often faced with harsh ultimatums: accept Islam, pay the jizya tax as nonbelievers, or risk military conquest and enslavement. While Islam brought unification and structure to many regions, it did so at the cost of countless indigenous spiritual systems that had thrived for centuries prior.

This historical context helps explain why paganism, once the dominant spiritual framework across much of the ancient world, is no longer widely visible today. Centuries of suppression, forced conversions, and cultural erasure led to the decline of traditional polytheistic practices and the rise of dominant monotheistic religions. Yet despite this, paganism never fully disappeared. Instead, it adapted and went underground, disguising itself within local customs, or surviving through oral traditions passed down in quiet defiance. Even today, millions of people around the world continue to practice these old ways in private. That being said, many of these pagans continue to hide their beliefs out of fear of social stigma, discrimination, or even political persecution, depending on where they live. In many cases, what may appear to be folklore or seasonal festivals are in fact echoes of much older pagan traditions that have persisted just beneath the surface of modern culture by those who practice in secret.

In fact, some of the most widely celebrated holidays in the modern world, particularly in the West, still carry unmistakable traces of their pagan origins. Christmas, for example, aligns closely with the ancient winter solstice festival of Yule, which was celebrated by Germanic and Norse pagans to mark the rebirth of the sun during the darkest time of year. Many familiar Christmas customs, such as decorating evergreen trees, hanging wreaths, burning yule logs, and even the figure of Santa Claus, have roots in pre-Christian winter rituals. Similarly, Easter coincides with ancient spring fertility festivals, especially those honoring goddesses like Ostara or Eostre. The use of eggs and rabbits, both symbols of rebirth and fertility, can be traced directly back to these earlier traditions. Although Christianity reinterpreted these festivals to align with its theological narratives, the seasonal rhythms and symbolic imagery of paganism remain deeply embedded in the way these holidays are celebrated today. This blending of traditions reveals just how resilient and enduring pagan practices have been, even after centuries of suppression.

While there are far too many forms of paganism to study in depth here, let's briefly explore some of the most well-known traditions to provide you with a foundational understanding. This will include ancient belief systems in Egyptian, Greek, Roman, Norse, and Celtic paganism. Each of these paths holds a rich tapestry of mythology, symbolism, rituals, and spiritual philosophies that continue to inspire people today. If one of these traditions sparks your curiosity, consider diving deeper into it. There is a wealth of knowledge available, thanks to historians, archaeologists, and spiritual practitioners who have devoted their lives to researching and preserving these sacred systems. Even if you don't believe in or practice any of these ancient traditions, exploring them can be a deeply enriching part of your spiritual journey.

Ancient Egypt

Ancient Egyptian religion is one of the oldest and most complex spiritual systems in human history. Known to its practitioners as the faith of Kemet, meaning "the Black Land," this term referred to the dark, fertile soil along the banks of the Nile River. The prosperity and order of Egyptian life were directly tied to the natural cycles of the Nile, and this deep connection to nature shaped their religious worldview. Spirituality was not a separate domain from daily existence, it was embedded into every facet of life. Natural events, political authority, social structure, and personal morality were all seen as expressions of divine will.

The Egyptian pantheon was immense and richly symbolic. Deities personified the forces of the universe and held distinct roles within a sacred cosmology. Ra, the solar god, traveled across the sky by day and journeyed through the underworld by night, bringing light and renewal. Osiris governed the afterlife and represented resurrection and judgment. Isis, one of the most beloved goddesses, embodied healing, protection, and magical knowledge. Horus was the divine protector of the pharaoh and symbolized kingship and celestial order. Thoth, god of wisdom, language, and time, was said to have created writing itself. These gods were not distant or metaphorical. They were understood as active presences that shaped the world and responded to ritual, prayer, and offerings.

Central to Egyptian religious philosophy was the principle of Ma'at. This was the concept of truth, justice, order, and cosmic harmony. Ma'at governed the movement of the stars, the balance of the seasons, and the integrity of human society. It was believed that maintaining Ma'at was necessary for the world to function correctly. The pharaoh, both a political and spiritual leader, was seen as the living embodiment of divine will and the upholder of Ma'at. Through temple building, just governance, warfare when required, and the enactment of sacred rites, the pharaoh played a crucial role in sustaining universal balance.

Temples were at the heart of religious life in Egypt. Far more than places of worship, they operated as centers of political authority, economic administration, medical care, education, and astronomical observation. Each temple housed a specific deity, whose presence was maintained through daily rituals performed by priests. These rituals included awakening the god's statue, cleansing and dressing it, offering food and incense, and reciting hymns. Only the priests could enter the innermost sanctuaries, but festivals and public processions allowed the wider population to participate in sacred events. Temple complexes were designed as symbolic models of the cosmos, reinforcing the relationship between divine order and human action.

Egyptian religious practice also heavily emphasized the afterlife. The journey of the soul after death was considered a sacred continuation of life on Earth. Texts such as the Pyramid Texts, Coffin Texts, and Book of the Dead provided spells, prayers, and moral guidance to help the deceased navigate the dangers of the underworld. Success in the afterlife depended on a person's ability to uphold Ma'at during their life and to pass the judgment of Osiris, who weighed their heart against the feather of truth.

Over time, Egyptian religion evolved as regional deities merged, foreign influences entered, and theological developments unfolded. One of the most significant transformations was the rise of Amun-Ra, a syncretic deity combining the Theban god Amun with the solar creator Ra. The cult of Amun grew so powerful that its priesthood held economic and political sway equal to the royal court during the New Kingdom. Despite such shifts, the foundational values of the religion, devotion to Ma'at, reverence for the gods, and the pursuit of eternal life, remained consistent for millennia.

The decline of traditional Egyptian religion began with foreign conquests. The Persians, Greeks, and later Romans gradually marginalized native practices, though many continued for centuries in both public and private forms. The final blow came with the spread of Christianity, which led to the closure of temples and the banning of pagan rituals by the fourth century CE. With these prohibitions, one of the world's longest-standing religious traditions came to an end, at least in its public expression.

In modern times, there has been a growing interest in reviving the ancient Egyptian faith through a movement known as Kemetism. Based on surviving inscriptions, archaeological research, and historical texts, modern practitioners seek to reconnect with the spiritual worldview of the ancient Egyptians. For them, it is not just a historical reenactment, but a way of life that emphasizes harmony with nature, respect for divine order, and honoring the ancestors. Thus, the echoes of Egyptian paganism continue to resonate with many today, offering timeless wisdom drawn from a civilization that saw the sacred in all things.

Ancient Greece

The spiritual worldview of ancient Greece is one of the most influential and well-documented polytheistic systems in history. It formed the foundation of Greek culture, politics, philosophy, and daily life for well over a thousand years, reaching its height between the eighth and fourth centuries BCE. At the heart of Greek paganism was a vast and intricate pantheon of gods and goddesses, each governing different aspects of nature, society, and the human condition. These deities were deeply anthropomorphic, possessing human emotions, desires, flaws, and virtues. As such, they were seen not only as divine but also as intimately relatable and involved in the lives of mortals.

The Olympian gods were considered the principal figures of this spiritual system. They resided on Mount Olympus, the mythical seat of the divine, and included Zeus, king of the gods and ruler of the sky; Hera, goddess of marriage and family; Poseidon, god of the sea and earthquakes; Demeter, goddess of agriculture and the harvest; Athena, guardian of wisdom and strategic warfare; Apollo, god of the sun, music, and prophecy; Artemis, huntress and protector of the wild; Ares, god of war; Aphrodite, goddess of love and beauty; Hephaestus, the divine smith and craftsman; Hermes, the messenger and guide of souls; and Dionysus, god of wine, ecstasy, and transformation. Each god had unique attributes, domains, stories, and symbols associated with them, and their worship varied from region to region.

Greek religion was not centralized. There was no single sacred text or ruling priesthood, and practices differed widely between city-states. Yet there was a shared cultural understanding of the gods and their stories that unified the Hellenic world. Public festivals and religious games were central to Greek life and served to honor the divine while also strengthening civic unity. Events such as the Olympic Games, held in honor of Zeus, combined athletic competition with sacred ritual. Similarly, the Panathenaia celebrated Athena with processions, sacrifices, and musical contests. These events provided much needed social cohesion between competing city states, even in times of intense political conflict.

Worship in ancient Greece took place both in grand temples and humble household shrines. Rituals included libations of wine, the burning of incense, prayers, hymns, and animal sacrifices. These offerings were believed to nourish the gods and establish reciprocity. Worshippers gave in order to receive favor, protection, or blessings. This concept of mutual exchange between mortals and gods shaped much of the religious mindset. Divine favor was sought not only for personal well-being, but also for success in agriculture, warfare, childbirth, and seafaring.

Temples were sacred spaces meant to house the presence of a deity. The innermost chamber, where the cult statue stood, was often restricted to priests and priestesses, while the public participated in outdoor rituals and feasts. Priests were not full-time spiritual leaders but often citizens appointed for limited terms. Their duties involved maintaining the temple, overseeing sacrifices, and ensuring the proper conduct of ceremonies. In many cases, women served as priestesses, particularly in the worship of goddesses such as Athena, Demeter, and Artemis.

Oracles played a central role in spiritual life. Among the most famous was the Oracle of Delphi, where a priestess known as the Pythia would deliver prophetic messages believed to come from Apollo. These oracles were consulted on matters ranging from personal concerns to major political decisions, and their influence shaped the course of Greek history. The Greeks viewed fate as a powerful and often inescapable force, and the gods were seen as both guides and enforcers of destiny.

Mythology provided the moral and spiritual framework of the Greek world. Myths explained the origins of the universe, the relationships among the gods, and the adventures of heroes. Figures such as Heracles, Perseus, Theseus, and Odysseus represented idealized traits like courage, cleverness, and resilience. Their stories were more than just entertainment. They were sacred narratives that carried ethical lessons and revealed the consequences of pride, disobedience, and imbalance to people of the ancient world. The myths explored many themes of transformation, loss, love, and renewal, offering spiritual insight through richly symbolic tales.

Greek thought did not always remain within the boundaries of myth. Philosophers began to explore deeper metaphysical questions about the nature of the divine, the soul, and the cosmos. While some thinkers, like Socrates and Plato, questioned literal interpretations of the gods, they still engaged deeply with spiritual ideas. Plato spoke of a realm of eternal forms, a kind of divine perfection beyond the material world. Aristotle proposed a prime mover, an unchanging force that caused all things to be. These ideas did not replace religion, but rather coexisted with traditional beliefs and helped shape later philosophical and theological systems.

In the centuries following Alexander the Great, Greek religion absorbed influences from Egypt, Persia, and other regions. This period saw the rise of mystery cults, esoteric spiritual traditions that offered initiates secret knowledge and promises of personal transformation. The Eleusinian Mysteries, dedicated to Demeter and Persephone, were among the most revered of these cults and offered hope for life beyond death. Other popular cults centered on Orpheus, Dionysus, and Isis, and emphasized purification, rebirth, and communion with the divine.

As the Roman Empire expanded and Christianity began to spread, traditional Greek religion gradually declined. Temples were closed, sacred texts were lost, and public worship was outlawed under Christian rule. Many deities were demonized or reinterpreted, and spiritual traditions that had endured for centuries were pushed underground or forgotten. Despite this, the influence of Greek paganism remained. Its symbols, stories, and values continued to shape Western art, literature, and philosophy for generations to come.

Today, a growing number of individuals have begun to explore Hellenism, a modern revival of ancient Greek religion. Based on classical texts, archaeological findings, and reconstructed rituals, these practitioners seek to reconnect with the wisdom of the old gods. For them, the Greek pantheon continues to represent timeless archetypes of natural forces. In honoring these gods, they aim to restore a sense of harmony with the earth, the cosmos, and the inner self.

Ancient Rome

Roman paganism was a vast and deeply rooted spiritual system that evolved over more than a thousand years, shaping the religious, political, and cultural life of ancient Rome. While often compared to the religion of ancient Greece due to its similar pantheon and mythology, Roman paganism was distinct in both its structure and emphasis. It was highly practical, civic-minded, and deeply intertwined with the Roman identity. Religion was not only a personal matter but a public duty. The success of the state was believed to depend directly on the proper veneration of the gods.

The Romans believed in a pantheon of gods and goddesses who governed all aspects of nature, society, and human endeavor. Many of these deities were adopted from earlier Italic traditions or borrowed from neighboring cultures. Later, as Rome came into contact with the Greeks, many Roman gods were associated with Greek counterparts, though their character and functions often remained uniquely Roman. Jupiter, the king of the gods, was associated with the sky and thunder, and became the chief deity of the Roman state. Juno, his consort, was the protector of women and marriage. Mars, originally a fertility god, evolved into the formidable god of war and became one of Rome's most honored figures. Venus embodied love and beauty, Mercury oversaw trade and communication, and Minerva represented wisdom and crafts.

Unlike the Greek gods, who were often depicted in myth as highly emotional and impulsive, the Roman gods were portrayed more as dignified and authoritative forces. Roman religion emphasized duty, discipline, and order. These values were reflected in their approach to worship, which was marked by ritual precision and formalism. Every prayer, sacrifice, or festival had to be conducted correctly, as any mistake was thought to offend the gods and risk divine punishment. The concept of *pax deorum*, meaning the peace of the gods, described the state of harmony between the divine and the human world. Maintaining this harmony was essential to Rome's continued prosperity.

Public religion was central to Roman life. The state employed a highly organized priesthood responsible for overseeing rituals, maintaining temples, and interpreting omens. Among the most important religious officials were the pontifices, who regulated the religious calendar and supervised sacred law. The flamines served as priests of individual gods, and the augurs interpreted signs from nature to determine divine favor. Perhaps the most revered religious order was the Vestal Virgins, priestesses of the goddess Vesta who tended the sacred fire of Rome. Their chastity and devotion were believed to safeguard the city, and their position carried immense honor and responsibility.

Temples were prominent in Roman cities and served not only as places of worship but also as symbols of civic pride and divine protection. These structures housed the images of the gods and served as the focal point for festivals and ceremonies. Important events such as military victories, imperial successions, or natural disasters were all marked by religious rites. Roman generals would offer sacrifices of gratitude after a campaign, and emperors often commissioned new temples to celebrate their divine favor.

Roman religion also included a rich tradition of household worship. Each family maintained a shrine, called a lararium, which honored protective spirits such as the Lares and Penates. These spirits were believed to safeguard the home and its inhabitants. Daily offerings and prayers were made to them, and significant life events such as births, marriages, and harvests were marked with private rituals. Ancestor worship was also important, with deceased relatives honored during festivals such as Parentalia, which served as a time to remember and nourish the spirits of the dead.

As the Roman Republic transitioned into the Roman Empire, religion became increasingly tied to imperial authority. Emperors were often deified after death, and in some cases, worshiped during their lifetimes. The imperial cult became a powerful tool for unifying the diverse peoples of the empire under a common system of loyalty and reverence. Temples to emperors were built throughout the provinces, and local communities were encouraged to participate in their veneration. While this form of worship was often more political than spiritual, it reflected the belief that divine favor was the key to Rome's continued dominance.

Roman paganism was also highly inclusive. As the empire expanded, Rome absorbed and adapted the deities of conquered peoples. Egyptian, Persian, and Celtic gods were often welcomed into the Roman pantheon, leading to a rich and diverse religious landscape. Mystery cults such as those of Isis, Mithras, and Cybele gained popularity, especially among soldiers and lower classes seeking personal salvation, initiation, and connection with the divine. These cults often promised rewards in the afterlife and emphasized inner transformation over public ritual.

The decline of Roman paganism began gradually with the rise of Christianity. While initially one of many mystery religions tolerated within the empire, Christianity's rapid growth eventually attracted suspicion and persecution. Over time, however, it gained favor among Roman elites and emperors. In the fourth century, Emperor Constantine legalized Christianity and began to support it publicly. His successors took further steps to suppress paganism. Temples were closed or repurposed, sacrifices were outlawed, and traditional rites were condemned as superstition or heresy.

By the end of the fifth century, Roman paganism had largely disappeared as a public religion. Yet many of its festivals, customs, and deities continued to influence later European culture. Elements of Roman religious practice were absorbed into Roman Catholic traditions, including the use of incense, candles, altars, and priestly garments. The Roman calendar, filled with pagan festivals, was restructured but never entirely erased. In literature, art, and philosophy, the gods of Rome remained a powerful source of inspiration.

Today, a growing number of people have begun to explore the old Roman religion under the name Religio Romana. Drawing from classical texts, archaeological records, and surviving ritual formulas, modern practitioners seek to honor the Roman gods and revive their traditional forms of worship. For many, it is not merely a historical exercise but a living spiritual path that emphasizes discipline, civic virtue, and reverence for the divine order. Roman paganism, with its deep respect for tradition, law, and the sacred rhythms of life, offers a spiritual vision grounded in the structure and advancement of human society.

The Celtic Druids

Celtic Druidry refers to the spiritual traditions practiced by the ancient Celtic peoples of Western Europe, particularly in regions that are today known as Ireland, Scotland, Wales, and parts of Gaul. Unlike the well-preserved mythologies of Greece and Rome, Celtic spiritual practices were largely oral, passed down through stories, songs, and ritual rather than written texts. As a result, much of what is known about Druidry comes from later medieval manuscripts and the accounts of Roman writers, who often viewed the Druids through the lens of conquest and suspicion. Despite this, the spiritual worldview of the Celts remains one of the most mysterious and evocative forms of ancient paganism.

At the heart of Celtic religion was a profound reverence for nature and its cycles. Sacred groves, rivers, hills, and stones were seen as dwellings of divine spirits. Trees, in particular, were held in great esteem. The oak, ash, and yew were considered especially sacred, often associated with wisdom, endurance, and the boundary between life and death. The natural world was not only inhabited by gods and spirits, but was itself considered divine. Every stream, glen, and mountain carried its own unique power and personality, which the Celtic people sought to live in harmony with.

The Druids were the priestly class of the Celts and served as intermediaries between the people and the divine. They were not only spiritual leaders but also scholars, healers, judges, poets, and advisors to kings. Their training was said to last for as long as twenty years, during which they memorized vast bodies of lore, astronomy, law, and ritual. Druids were revered for their wisdom and held significant influence over both religious and political matters. They conducted public ceremonies, interpreted omens, offered sacrifices, and presided over seasonal festivals that marked the turning of the year.

Celtic mythology was rich with gods, goddesses, and heroic figures who embodied the forces of nature, war, love, fertility, and transformation. These deities were not confined to distant heavens but were seen as actively present in the land and the lives of the people. The Morrigan, for example, was a goddess of battle, fate, and sovereignty, often appearing as a raven on the battlefield. Brigid was a beloved goddess of healing, poetry, and the hearth, later transformed into a Christian saint. Lugh was a solar hero associated with craftsmanship, skill, and leadership. The gods of the Celts were deeply interconnected with the stories of heroes and ancestors, forming a cosmology rooted in both myth and lineage.

The wheel of the year was central to Celtic spirituality. This cycle included major festivals such as Samhain, the end of the harvest and the beginning of winter, when the veil between the worlds was believed to be thinnest. Beltane, celebrated at the start of summer, was a festival of fertility and fire. Imbolc marked the first signs of spring and was associated with purification and renewal, while Lughnasadh honored the grain harvest and the sun god Lugh. These festivals were not only agricultural markers but sacred times when the community gathered to celebrate, give thanks, and commune with the unseen world.

Burial practices and beliefs about the afterlife also played a significant role in Celtic religion. The Celts believed in a soul that continued after death, often journeying to the Otherworld, a realm of beauty, abundance, and eternal youth. This world was not separate from the mortal one but existed alongside it, accessible through sacred sites, dreams, or altered states of consciousness. Burial mounds, stone circles, and caves were seen as thresholds to the Otherworld, and many rituals were designed to honor ancestors and seek guidance from the spirits of the dead.

The coming of the Romans and later the spread of Christianity brought about the suppression and eventual disappearance of the public practice of Druidry. Roman accounts describe campaigns specifically aimed at eradicating the Druids, whom they viewed as politically and spiritually subversive. Sacred groves were cut down, and oral traditions were lost or transformed. However, elements of Druidic belief survived in the folk traditions of Celtic regions, hidden in the stories, festivals, and healing practices of rural communities.

Medieval Irish manuscripts such as the *Lebor Gabála Érenn* and the *Mabinogion* preserved echoes of the old myths, though often reinterpreted through a Christian lens.

In modern times, there has been a revival of interest in Celtic spirituality through the contemporary Druidic movement. Known as Neo-Druidry, this path seeks to reconstruct and reimagine ancient druidic practices in a modern context. While it is impossible to recreate the original Druidic tradition in full, modern Druids draw inspiration from mythology, archaeology, folklore, and the rhythms of the natural world. Many practice seasonal rituals, study the Ogham tree alphabet, and work with the spirits of land and ancestors. The focus is often on personal growth, environmental stewardship, and spiritual connection to the cycles of life.

Celtic Druidry offers a tangible form of spirituality that is deeply rooted in the earth, shaped by story and symbol, and centered on the interconnectedness of all life. It teaches reverence for the land, respect for wisdom, and the importance of honoring both the past and the present. For those seeking a path that values mystery, nature, and ancestral memory, the tradition of the Druids continues to whisper through the forests and stones of the Celtic lands, inviting a return to sacred relationship with the world.

The Norse

Norse paganism refers to the ancient spiritual traditions practiced by the Germanic and Scandinavian peoples of Northern Europe, particularly in regions that are now known as Norway, Sweden, Denmark, and Iceland. Sometimes called the Old Norse religion, this system of belief was rooted in a deep connection to nature, fate, and the heroic spirit. It flourished from the early centuries of the Common Era until the Christianization of the North in the late medieval period. Although much of what is known about Norse paganism comes from medieval Icelandic sources written after the arrival of Christianity, these texts preserve a strikingly rich and coherent worldview that continues to inspire fascination to this day.

At the heart of Norse cosmology was Yggdrasil, the World Tree, an immense ash that connected the nine realms of existence. These realms included Asgard, the home of the gods; Midgard, the world of humans; and Helheim, the underworld of the dead. The universe was seen as a vast and living structure, ordered yet subject to constant change. Fate, known as Wyrd or Orlog, was an inescapable force woven by the Norns, three mysterious figures who spun the threads of destiny. Even the gods themselves were bound by fate and were aware that their end would come in a future event known as Ragnarok.

The Norse pantheon was divided into two major groups of deities: the Aesir and the Vanir. The Aesir were gods of power, law, war, and rulership, and included figures such as Odin, the Allfather and god of wisdom, magic, and the dead. Thor, the thunder god and protector of humanity, was revered for his strength and courage. Frigg, the wife of Odin, was a goddess of foresight and family. The Vanir were associated with fertility, nature, and prosperity. Among them were Njord, the god of the sea and wealth, and his children Freyr and Freyja, who represented abundance, love, and sacred sexuality. The two clans of gods were once at war but eventually made peace, symbolizing the balance between order and nature.

Norse mythology is filled with stories of gods, giants, heroes, and mythical beasts, often told through epic poems and sagas. These tales reveal a worldview that embraced struggle, courage, and the inevitability of death. Heroes such as Sigurd, Brynhild, and Ragnar Lodbrok were celebrated not for perfect virtue, but for their ability to face fate with honor. Even the gods were not immortal in the absolute sense. They could suffer, make mistakes, and ultimately fall. Yet their persistence in the face of doom gave them nobility. This emphasis on honor in the face of inevitable decline gave Norse spirituality a unique character, one that valued resilience, loyalty, and the acceptance of life's harsh truths.

Religious practice in Norse society was community-based and centered around seasonal festivals, sacred sites, and household rituals. Blóts, or sacrificial feasts, were held to honor the gods, spirits, and ancestors. These ceremonies involved offerings of animals, food, drink, and sometimes even weapons or personal treasures. Sacred groves, stones, and springs served as natural temples, while large feasting halls and mead gatherings provided the social setting for communal worship. The gods were not seen as distant, abstract beings, but as powerful presences woven into the world. By giving offerings and performing rites, Norse people sought to maintain balance with these forces and ensure good fortune in battle, harvest, or travel.

Another central aspect of Norse spirituality was the veneration of ancestors. The dead were believed to remain active within the community as protectors, guides, or even as beings who needed continued care. Burial mounds and grave goods were prepared with great attention, reflecting a belief in an afterlife that was both physical and spiritual. The concept of Valhalla, the hall of the slain, was reserved for warriors who died bravely in battle and were taken by the Valkyries to feast with Odin until the end of the world. Others might journey to Helheim, a quieter realm of the dead ruled by the goddess Hel. While later sources made distinctions between these destinations, it is likely that beliefs about the afterlife varied widely across time and region.

Magic, known as Seidr, played a vital role in Norse religious life. This form of sorcery was associated with prophecy, shapeshifting, and communication with the unseen. It was often practiced by women known as Volvas or seeresses, who entered trance states to speak with spirits or see into the threads of fate. Odin himself was said to have practiced Seidr, although this was considered an unusual and even taboo behavior for men, as Seidr was often viewed as a feminine power. Runes also held magical significance, not only as a writing system, but as symbols imbued with sacred meaning. The act of carving runes into wood or stone was thought to invoke spiritual power or bring about change in the world.

The Christianization of Scandinavia began in the ninth century and unfolded over several generations. Missionaries, kings, and foreign powers gradually replaced Norse religious structures with

Christian institutions. Temples were dismantled or repurposed, sacred groves were cut down, and stories were rewritten to align with new religious teachings. Despite this, many elements of Norse mythology have survived in folklore, local customs, and even in Christian stories adapted for Northern Europeans. The myths preserved in the *Poetic Edda* and *Prose Edda*, written in Iceland during the thirteenth century, ensured that the gods of Asgard would be remembered throughout history.

In modern times, Norse paganism has seen a revival through spiritual movements like Heathenry or Ásatrú. These contemporary paths seek to reconstruct and reimagine the ancient faith using historical texts, archaeology, and Northern tradition. Modern practitioners typically honor the Norse gods and goddesses through seasonal festivals, rituals, and offerings. Many also place strong emphasis on community, personal honor, and a deep connection to ancestors and nature. While some groups focus on cultural heritage, many still see the Norse gods as living archetypes of humanity to be worshipped.

Norse paganism offers a holistic vision of the world as a place of beauty, struggle, and interconnectedness. It invites its followers to face life with courage, to walk with the ancestors, and to honor the sacred, despite all the challenges you may face. For those drawn to a path of strength, myth, and meaning rooted in the land and the cycles of nature, the old Norse faith continues to offer a thriving community to engage with.

6

MONOTHEISM

As the old pagan traditions declined and empires expanded, a new spiritual model took hold, centered on a single, all-powerful deity. This marked the rise of monotheism, defined as the belief in one god as the sole creator and ruler of the universe. While animism and paganism focused on relationships with nature and local deities, monotheistic religions emphasized moral order, divine revelation, and obedience to a singular divine will. Today, the world's largest religions (Judaism, Christianity, and Islam) are all monotheistic, shaping the spiritual lives of billions.

While I will not devote as much space to the major monotheistic religions as I did to pagan traditions, this is not a reflection of their importance. Rather, it is because these religions already possess extensive sacred texts and theological works that outline their beliefs in great detail. One could easily spend a lifetime studying the Bible, the Quran, or the Talmud and still only scratch the surface of their depth and complexity. Instead, what follows is a brief overview of monotheistic traditions, their core teachings, and the ways in which magic or mystical practice appears within them.

Judaism

Judaism is one of the oldest surviving monotheistic religions, emerging over three thousand years ago in the ancient Near East. Central to Jewish belief is the idea of a covenant, which maintains a sacred agreement between the Hebrew people and a singular, invisible God known as Yahweh. This God is not represented by idols or images but is understood through teachings, commandments, and sacred texts.

The Hebrew Bible, particularly the Torah, outlines both religious laws and historical narratives, including the Exodus from Egypt and the giving of the Ten Commandments at Mount Sinai. Jewish practice emphasizes community, ethical living, study, and remembrance of God's role in history. Observances like Shabbat, Passover, and Yom Kippur are deeply symbolic, serving as ritual reminders of divine presence and justice.

Though Judaism does not center magic in the way that pagan or occult traditions do, it has mystical branches, especially Kabbalah. Kabbalists view the universe as a series of emanations from the divine, structured by sacred patterns and numerology. They study hidden meanings in scripture and may use sacred letters, names, or symbols to connect with higher realms. Kabbalah is not practiced by all Jews, but it remains one of the most influential mystical systems in Western spirituality.

Christianity

Christianity arose in the first century of the common era, emerging from Jewish traditions and centered around the life, death, and resurrection of Jesus of Nazareth, who is regarded as the divine Son of God. Christians believe that Jesus' sacrifice atoned for humanity's sins, offering a path to salvation and eternal life through faith, grace, and moral living.

The Christian Bible includes the Old Testament, shared with Judaism, and the New Testament, which contains the teachings of

Jesus and his early followers. Core Christian beliefs include the Trinity, the forgiveness of sins, and the importance of love, compassion, and service to others.

Although Christianity explicitly condemns magical practice, its rituals share many features with magical systems. Baptism, anointing, communion, exorcisms, and blessings are ritual acts meant to invoke divine power and transformation. In the medieval period, Christian mystics reported visions, healings, and ecstatic encounters with angels and saints. Christian mysticism developed its own spiritual disciplines such as contemplative prayer, fasting, and the use of sacred symbols like the cross.

Certain folk traditions, such as Catholic folk magic or grimoire-based Christianity, preserved a blend of Christian imagery with magical ritual. These practices often involved psalms, saints, and holy relics as tools of spiritual influence. Though controversial within church doctrine, they show how deeply interwoven spirituality and magic have remained throughout history.

Catholicism

As the oldest and most ritualized branch of Christianity, Catholicism developed a rich spiritual culture that blends formal doctrine with layers of symbol, sacrament, and mystery. Rooted in the early Church and shaped by centuries of theological councils, monastic traditions, and imperial patronage, Catholicism views itself as the original guardian of Christian truth. It places strong emphasis on apostolic succession, sacred tradition, and the authority of the Pope as the earthly representative of Christ.

Catholic spiritual life is structured around the seven sacraments, which are seen as outward signs of inward grace. These include baptism, confirmation, Eucharist, confession, anointing of the sick, marriage, and holy orders. Each carries deep symbolic weight and is believed to enact real spiritual transformation. The Mass, in particular, is the central ritual of Catholic worship, where bread and wine are believed to become the literal body and blood of Christ through the mystery of transubstantiation.

Catholicism also embraces a vivid cosmology filled with saints, angels, and martyrs. Devotion to Mary, the mother of Jesus, is especially prominent, with prayers like the rosary and feast days honoring her role as intercessor. Statues, relics, candles, incense, and holy water are all used in devotional practice, creating a tangible and sensory spiritual experience. It is not uncommon in Catholicism for people to ask saints or angels to pray on their behalf, adding spiritual weight to their prayers.

Though official doctrine condemns sorcery and occultism, Catholicism has long coexisted with magical folk practices in the cultures it influenced. In many parts of Europe and Latin America, Catholic saints became syncretized with older deities or local spirits, forming a complex spiritual landscape where church teachings blended with ancestral traditions. Folk Catholicism includes blessings, home altars, novenas, and the use of charms, herbs, and prayers for healing and protection. In these traditions, magic is fully embraced as a tool for spiritual growth in Christianity.

Islam

Islam was founded in the seventh century in Arabia by the prophet Muhammad, who Muslims believe received divine revelations from God through the angel Gabriel. These revelations would ultimately become the Quran, Islam's central holy text. Islam emphasizes the oneness of God, the importance of living a righteous life, and the pursuit of submission to divine will through the Five Pillars. These include faith, prayer, charity, fasting, and pilgrimage to Mecca.

Islam discourages the use of magic, especially if it involves invoking spirits or straying from divine will. However, the Islamic world has a rich tradition of mysticism, most notably through Sufism. Sufis seek inner union with God through music, poetry, meditation, and devotion. Practices like dhikr, which involve the chanting of

God's names and whirling dances, are designed to awaken spiritual ecstasy and presence.

There are also traditional systems of Islamic astrology, numerology, and healing, particularly in North Africa, Persia, and South Asia. While not officially endorsed by Islamic scholars, these traditions survive as a form of spiritual folk wisdom that blends the sacred and the practical.

Magic in Monotheism

While monotheistic religions often reject magic in an official sense, magical thinking persists within them. The use of holy water, blessings, prayers, relics, and sacred words can all be seen as magical acts. These are intentional efforts to interact with the unseen, shaped by spiritual belief and ritualized action. The difference lies largely in framing. Acts done through the will of God are considered acceptable, while those done outside of that divine authority are condemned.

Each of the major monotheistic religions also has mystical or esoteric branches that blur the line between religion and magic. Whether through Kabbalah, Christian mysticism, or Sufism, these traditions share the same human longing for transformation, connection, and the direct experience of the sacred. Even within the most structured religious systems, the desire to know the divine personally and powerfully remains.

7

KARMA

In any exploration of spiritual or magical practice, one concept continues to surface across cultures and belief systems: the idea that your actions carry consequences. Known in Sanskrit as karma, this principle holds that every choice you make creates an energetic imprint that eventually returns to you, whether in this life or beyond. Karma is an intricate law of cause and effect that invites you to reflect on the deeper currents behind your intentions, habits, and behaviors.

The concept of karma has roots in ancient Indian philosophy, particularly within Hinduism, Buddhism, Jainism, and later Sikhism. In each tradition, karma is closely tied to the soul's journey, moral conduct, and the cycle of rebirth, known as samsara. While interpretations vary, the core message remains the same: your thoughts, words, and deeds shape your reality. You are not a passive recipient of fate, but an active participant in its unfolding.

Karma in Hinduism

In Hindu philosophy, karma is part of a broader spiritual system involving dharma (righteous duty), artha (material success), kama (desire), and moksha (liberation). Karma governs the spiritual ledger of your actions. Good deeds, performed with sincerity and without selfishness, contribute to positive karma. Harmful actions, particularly those driven by greed, hatred, or ignorance, generate negative karma. This karmic balance influences not only your current life circumstances, but also the conditions of future incarnations.

However, karma is not always immediate. It unfolds according to divine timing, shaped by layers of past choices and deeper lessons the soul must learn. A person may be born into hardship not as a punishment, but as an opportunity to grow, repay a past debt, or break an old cycle.

Karma in Buddhism

Buddhism approaches karma with a slightly different lens. It teaches that karma is not enforced by any god or supernatural being, but is simply a natural law. The focus is not on judgment, but on awareness and intention. Each action you take is like planting a seed. Over time, that seed grows into experience. If your actions are rooted in compassion, wisdom, and mindfulness, the fruits will be peace and clarity. If they are rooted in craving, ignorance, or hatred, they will bring suffering and confusion.

Importantly, Buddhism emphasizes the role of the mind in karmic creation. Thoughts, just like deeds, have power. A hateful thought may not harm another person directly, but it conditions your own mind, making anger more likely to arise again. Over time, these patterns become your reality.

Some schools of Buddhism, especially in the Vajrayana and Mahayana traditions, also explore karma through the lens of compassionate action. They emphasize the importance of purifying karma through right living, spiritual practice, and self-inquiry. Even harmful past actions are thought to be transformed through sincere reflection and ethical conduct moving forward.

Karma in Western Spirituality

Although the concept of karma originated from Eastern traditions, similar ideas have long existed within Western spiritual frameworks, particularly in the form of divine justice, moral consequence, and spiritual reciprocity. In Christianity, for example, the idea that "you reap what you sow" (Galatians 6:7) echoes the karmic belief that one's actions eventually return in kind. While framed in terms of divine will rather than cosmic law, this principle still teaches that good actions lead to blessings, while harmful ones lead to suffering.

In Western magical traditions, this concept often surfaces through beliefs such as the Threefold Law or the Rule of Return, which suggest that the energy you send into the world, whether through thought, action, or spellwork, will eventually come back to you multiplied. Though not universally accepted among practitioners of magic, this belief acts as an ethical guidepost. It discourages acts of harm, manipulation, or vengeance and encourages practitioners to align their magic with healing, growth, and personal responsibility.

Even outside of formal religion or magic, Western culture often reflects a karmic mindset in sayings like "what goes around comes around" or the golden rule: "treat others as you wish to be treated." These reflect a deep-rooted intuition that actions have consequences, not just externally, but spiritually and psychologically. In this way, karma also aligns with the magical principle of correspondence: "as within, so without." The energy you hold internally shapes your experience of the outer world. A practitioner filled with resentment may notice more conflict and difficulty in their life, while one who cultivates compassion and integrity often finds greater peace and synchronicity.

Whether understood as divine justice, energetic balance, or psychological mirroring, the Western expression of karma serves as a powerful reminder that your actions matter. Not just because of how they affect others, but because of how they shape the person you are becoming and the spiritual path you walk.

Living with Karmic Awareness

Karma is not meant to inspire guilt, fear, or fatalism. It is not divine revenge, nor a cosmic tally of moral points. It is a reflection of the ongoing relationship between choice and consequence. Every act plants a seed. Every thought forms a pattern. What you nurture grows.

This means karma is not fixed. It can be shaped, healed, and transformed. Through awareness, meditation, shadow work, forgiveness, and ethical living, karmic patterns can be disrupted. Even ancient burdens passed down through ancestral lines can be transmuted with compassion and courage. This is why some practitioners include karmic cleansing rituals in their work, seeking to release inherited or accumulated patterns that no longer serve them.

In your spiritual or magical practice, you will inevitably be faced with moments of choice, whether to act with grace or with anger, to protect or to punish, to control or to let go. In these moments, the principle of karma invites you to pause and reflect. What energy are you invoking? What seeds are you planting? Are you creating more suffering, or breaking a cycle?

This does not mean you must always be passive or forgiving. Sometimes the most karmically aligned path is one of clear boundaries, protection, and justice. But even then, intention matters. Are you acting from love, or from revenge? Are you seeking healing, or causing harm?

Karma teaches us that we are always shaping the path beneath our feet. It is not a distant cosmic law, but a living current woven into every choice you make. When practiced with awareness, karma becomes not a burden, but a guide. It reminds you that you are never powerless. With every thought and deed, you are writing your own future.

8

THE AFTERLIFE

W hat happens after we die? This question has echoed through every civilization, belief system, and sacred text. For some, the soul moves on to paradise or judgment. For others, it returns again and again in a cycle of growth, rebirth, and spiritual evolution. The concept of an afterlife, whether eternal or cyclical, has provided humanity with a framework to understand death, morality, and the deeper meaning of life.

While some traditions describe a singular post-death destination, many offer a more layered view of the soul's journey. Reincarnation is one such vision, in which the soul does not perish with the body but is reborn into new circumstances, shaped by the actions and intentions of earlier lives. In other systems, the soul undergoes judgment, ascends to a divine realm, or gradually merges with a higher state of consciousness. Understanding these ideas provides more than just religious insight. It helps us reflect on how we live, how we interpret suffering, and how we make sense of death.

Reincarnation in Hinduism

In Hindu philosophy, the soul, known as the atman, is considered eternal and divine. It is believed to cycle through countless births and deaths within the realm of samsara, which refers to the repeating cycle of earthly existence. This cycle is propelled by karma, the principle of cause and effect based on one's actions, thoughts, and intentions.

Each incarnation presents a new opportunity to fulfill one's dharma, or sacred duty, and to purify the soul through ethical living and spiritual discipline. When a soul has completed its learning, it can attain moksha, or liberation from the cycle of reincarnation. Moksha is not a place but a state of unity with Brahman, the universal divine source. In this view, the afterlife is not a final destination, but part of a larger cosmic process of soul development.

Reincarnation in Buddhism

Buddhism teaches a concept of rebirth similar to Hinduism but with an important distinction. It does not view the soul as a permanent entity. Instead, what continues is a stream of consciousness shaped by karma and mental formations. This consciousness takes on a new form after death, and the process continues until enlightenment is reached.

The ultimate goal in Buddhism is to attain nirvana, a state beyond suffering and rebirth. In Tibetan Buddhism, teachings describe an intermediate state between lives called the bardo. This is a liminal space where the soul encounters various visions and opportunities for liberation. Some advanced practitioners, such as Tibetan lamas, are believed to reincarnate intentionally to continue their spiritual mission. These reincarnated teachers are called tulkus and are often recognized during early childhood.

Reincarnation in Jainism and Sikhism

Jainism also teaches reincarnation, with an emphasis on the soul's need for liberation through nonviolence, detachment, and self-discipline. Every action binds karmic matter to the soul, and the ultimate goal is to become free from all attachments and attain a state of perfect knowledge and bliss.

Sikhism, which shares some of the cosmological ideas of Hinduism, acknowledges the cycle of rebirth but focuses more strongly on union with the divine. Liberation is achieved through devotion to God, selfless service, remembrance of divine truth, and moral living. Reincarnation is seen as a consequence of spiritual separation, and the soul returns to Earth until it becomes absorbed in God's presence.

The Afterlife in Abrahamic Religions

Judaism holds diverse views of the afterlife. Early Hebrew texts describe Sheol as a shadowy place where the dead reside. Later writings introduce the idea of resurrection and a future world to come. In Jewish mysticism, especially in Kabbalah, there is a belief in gilgul, the transmigration of souls. Souls may return to Earth to complete spiritual tasks or rectify past imbalances.

Christianity traditionally teaches that the soul faces judgment after death and proceeds to either Heaven or Hell. The Catholic tradition includes the idea of Purgatory, a place of purification for those not yet ready for Heaven. Some early Christian sects and mystics, including the theologian Origen, taught that souls pre-existed and could return after death, though these ideas were eventually deemed heretical by the institutional Church.

Islam offers a rich and detailed account of the afterlife. Upon death, the soul enters a state of waiting called Barzakh. After resurrection, all souls are judged based on their deeds. The righteous are rewarded with eternal life in Paradise, while others are cast into Hell. Although Islam does not support the idea of reincarnation, Sufi mystics have described spiritual ascension through various planes of existence and have emphasized the soul's journey back to God.

Indigenous and Pagan Perspectives on Death

In many Indigenous cultures, the afterlife is deeply connected to the land, the ancestors, and the spirit world. Death is not an ending but a transition into another phase of being. The soul may remain as a guiding presence, reincarnate within the family line, or travel to a sacred realm of spirits.

In ancient Greece, philosophers like Plato and Pythagoras described a soul that reincarnates in pursuit of wisdom and purity. Plato wrote about the soul choosing its next life based on the lessons it still needs to learn. Mystery traditions, such as those practiced at Eleusis, aimed to prepare the soul for its journey beyond death.

In Norse mythology, the soul could go to Valhalla, Helheim, or other spiritual destinations depending on one's life and manner of death. While reincarnation was not a central belief, there was recognition of spiritual continuity and fate.

Celtic Druidry embraced a belief in the soul's return to Earth. It was thought that souls could reincarnate multiple times, often within their community or tribe, and that the afterlife was simply another part of a continuous cycle of existence.

The Journey of Souls

Modern explorations of the afterlife often center around spiritual regression and intuitive recall. One of the most influential works in this field is *Journey of Souls* by Dr. Michael Newton, a hypnotherapist who used deep-regression techniques to explore the space between incarnations. According to the consistent accounts of his clients, the soul enters a non-physical realm after death where it is met by guides, reviews its past life, reconnects with soul groups, and prepares for the next incarnation.

Rather than being judged or punished, souls are said to reflect on the impact of their actions and choose future circumstances that will help them grow. This view sees life as a sacred learning process. Challenges are not accidents but agreed-upon experiences that assist in healing and development. Souls often reincarnate with members of their soul group in different roles, helping one another through many lifetimes.

Other researchers, like Dr. Ian Stevenson, investigated cases of young children who recalled specific past lives. These children often knew names, locations, and details they had no normal way of learning. While not universally accepted by science, the consistency of these cases suggests the possibility of memory or consciousness continuing beyond a single lifetime.

Past Life Regression Theory

Past life regression is a therapeutic and spiritual practice used to explore memories or impressions believed to originate from previous incarnations. It typically involves a deeply relaxed meditative or hypnotic state in which the conscious mind steps aside, allowing deeper layers of memory to emerge. These experiences may manifest as visions, feelings, or spontaneous storytelling.

Practitioners believe that many psychological patterns, such as irrational fears, recurring dreams, or sudden emotional reactions, may originate from experiences in prior lives. By bringing these memories to light, individuals can release unresolved pain, understand karmic patterns, and reclaim personal power.

Some regressions reveal traumatic events that help explain present emotional wounds. Others may uncover past-life talents, spiritual roles, or deep connections with people in one's current life. In some cases, clients report profound healing or closure after a single session.

Skeptics argue that these experiences may be symbolic or imaginative rather than literal. But even as a metaphor, past life regression can offer valuable insight. Whether viewed as spiritual memory or unconscious storytelling, it often illuminates the deeper threads of a person's identity and purpose.

Working with past lives is ultimately about understanding the forces that have shaped you and using that awareness to grow. It serves as a potent reminder that you are part of a greater story, a soul in motion, weaving through lifetimes in search of truth, love, and wholeness like everybody else.

SECTION II:

FOUNDATIONS OF MAGIC

"Magic is the art of transforming consciousness according to will."

— Dion Fortune

WITCHCRAFT

B y the Middle Ages, paganism had been largely suppressed throughout Europe and North Africa. The old gods had been replaced by dominant monotheistic faiths, and those who continued to follow ancestral traditions were forced to adapt their practices in secrecy without the use of pagan idols. In this environment, a quiet transformation began to take place. Elements of European folk magic, herbal healing, and seasonal rituals blended into what would eventually become known as witchcraft. For centuries, it has been feared, romanticized, and misunderstood. But long before it was seen as rebellion or heresy, witchcraft was simply a way of working with the natural world to influence reality. At its heart, witchcraft has always been about healing, survival, and spiritual connection.

Long before the term "witch" took on its negative connotations, people across Europe practiced forms of folk magic that were deeply rooted in local customs. These individuals, sometimes called "wise women," "cunning folk," or "healers," held vital roles in their communities. They were herbalists, midwives, charm-makers, and protectors of the household. Their knowledge was passed down orally, tied to the land, and often interwoven with pre-Christian beliefs about spirits, ancestors, and natural cycles. These practices were neither centralized nor dogmatic. They varied from village to village and were shaped by the seasons, the local environment, and the needs of the people. A charm to protect livestock, a tincture to ease childbirth, or a ritual to bless a new home. These were all part of everyday magic, integrated into the rhythms of life.

For many years, witchcraft was largely tolerated by society despite the persecution of pagans, as it often blended with elements of Christianity or lacked obvious signs of idol worship. It was more often viewed as a profession rather than a religious system, and thus it did not threaten the monotheistic beliefs of the time. That all changed with the rise of institutional religion and the centralized political power of the Catholic Church. Beginning in the late medieval period, witchcraft became a target of suspicion and control. As Christianity spread across Europe, practices that didn't conform to church doctrine were increasingly labeled as heretical or dangerous. By the 15th century, fears of devil worship and spiritual corruption began to take hold, leading to centuries of brutal persecution.

The European witch hunts, reaching their peak between the 15th and 17th centuries, were not isolated or random. They were driven by religious extremism, social paranoia, and the desire to suppress marginalized groups, especially women. Women who were poor, widowed, unmarried, or simply different were particularly vulnerable to accusation. Those who practiced folk healing, owned land, or refused to conform to patriarchal expectations were often the first to be accused of consorting with the devil.

The legal and religious systems of the time legitimized these fears, with manuals like the *Malleus Maleficarum* instructing inquisitors on how to identify and punish witches. Torture, forced confessions, and public executions became common. By the end of the witch trial era, tens of thousands of people had been killed, and countless more had suffered under suspicion and fear. In reality, most of those accused were innocent of any wrongdoing beyond existing on the fringes of society.

Yet witchcraft did not vanish. Despite the violence, many of its core traditions endured, hidden in rural customs, folk medicine, seasonal festivals, and family superstitions. What the authorities tried to destroy was never a single, organized religion, but rather a vast and diverse collection of ancestral wisdom. These practices lived on in whispers, in gardens, in kitchen rituals, and in the passing of knowledge from grandmother to granddaughter.

Wicca and the Modern Revival

In the 20th century, witchcraft began to reemerge in public consciousness, not as a crime, but as a spiritual path. Much of this modern revival can be traced to the birth of Wicca, a contemporary pagan religion founded by Gerald Gardner in the 1950s. Drawing from ceremonial magic, British folklore, Eastern philosophy, and his own experiences within esoteric circles, Gardner introduced a system of witchcraft that blended ancient themes with modern sensibilities.

Wicca is a nature-based religion that honors both a God and a Goddess as two aspects of divine polarity. It emphasizes seasonal cycles, personal growth, and harmony with the earth. Its ritual calendar is centered around the Wheel of the Year, a cycle of eight Sabbats that celebrate the changing seasons and agricultural milestones, including Samhain, Imbolc, Beltane, and Lammas. These festivals are drawn from older European pagan traditions but reinterpreted for modern practitioners.

Unlike the fear-based narratives of the past, Wicca promotes a positive and ethical form of magic. Its central moral guideline, the Wiccan Rede, states: *"An it harm none, do what ye will."* This philosophy encourages freedom of practice, provided it does not bring harm to others. Wiccans often work with elemental energies, cast protective circles, and perform spells for healing, clarity, abundance, and connection. They may use tools such as candles, herbs, crystals, and ritual objects, but it is *intention* that fuels their magic, not the items themselves.

Wicca also popularized the idea of covens, which are small, organized groups of witches who meet regularly for ritual, study, and celebration. However, not all Wiccans belong to covens. Many practice as solitaries, crafting their own rituals and spiritual routines in private. The religion is flexible, open-ended, and deeply personal, which is one of the reasons it has gained such a broad following around the world.

Today, Wicca is just one of many expressions of modern witchcraft. Some practitioners follow it closely as a structured spiritual path, while others draw from it more loosely, blending its teachings with other traditions. Many choose not to use any specific label at all. Not all witches are Wiccan, and not all Wiccans identify as witches. The two are related, but they are not the same. If you feel drawn to working with deities and celebrating the cycles of nature through ritual, Wicca may resonate with you. It offers a blend of religious paganism and magical practice. However, if you are more interested in spells, energy work, and personal intention without involving deities or spiritual belief systems, then you may be more aligned with witchcraft as a practice rather than a religion.

RITUAL TOOLS

Throughout history, ritual tools have played a central role in magical and spiritual practices across nearly every culture. These objects are not inherently magical on their own. Rather, they serve as conduits for intention, energy, and symbolic focus. When used with clarity and purpose, ritual tools can transform an ordinary act into a sacred one. They help the practitioner enter a ritual mindset, create energetic boundaries, and connect with unseen forces. Whether you are casting a spell, honoring a deity, or simply manifesting an intention, your tools help shape the ritual into something meaningful and effective.

What we recognize today as tools of ritual magic have roots in many ancient spiritual traditions across the world, where objects like wands, blades, and sacred herbs were used for their symbolic meaning. Ancient Egyptians used wands made from ivory or copper to direct energy in temple rites. In Greece and Rome, ceremonial knives and incense burners were used in public rituals and household offerings. Indigenous communities often used feathers, stones, rattles, or bundles of sacred herbs in healing ceremonies. Over time, these instruments evolved, blended, and adapted to form the core ritual toolkit still used by modern witches, ceremonial magicians, and spiritual practitioners today.

You do not need to possess an elaborate collection of ritual tools to begin your magical practice. In fact, some of the most powerful rituals use no physical tools at all. What matters most is your relationship to any tools you do use. Treat them with respect, store them with care, and use them with clear intention. Over time, they will become more than just objects. They will become extensions of your will, mirrors of your energy, and trusted companions on your spiritual path.

As you build your collection, allow it to grow organically. Let yourself be drawn to the tools that speak to you. Whether found in nature, passed down from family, or purchased with purpose, your tools will carry the energy you put into them. Together, they form the bones of your ritual practice and help you turn ordinary moments into sacred acts of magic.

Below is an overview of the most commonly used ritual tools and their symbolic significance. These are not required to practice magic, but understanding them can help you develop your own intuitive relationship with your spiritual work.

The Wand

The wand is a tool of direction and intention. It is used to channel and project energy, especially when casting ritual circles or invoking elemental forces. Traditionally associated with the element of air, the wand can also represent fire in some traditions. It is often made from wood, particularly from the branches of trees believed to hold magical properties, like the willow, oak, ash, or elder tree.

Historically, wands appear in the hands of priests, pharaohs, and sages as instruments of spiritual authority. In modern magical practice, they are commonly used to trace symbols in the air, direct the flow of energy, or invite deities and spirits into sacred space. Your wand does not need to be elaborate. A simple, polished stick found in nature can be just as powerful as a carved or gem-encrusted one, so long as it is treated with respect.

The Athame

The athame is a ritual knife, often with a black handle, used to cut energetic boundaries and symbolize the power of the will. Unlike a physical knife used for practical cutting, the athame is rarely used to cut physical objects. Instead, it is used to direct force, sever attachments, or draw symbols like the pentagram during ritual.

It is often associated with the element of fire or air depending on the tradition, and is considered a masculine or projective tool. The origins of the athame are debated, but it is likely that it evolved from ceremonial blades used in early religious rites. In some paths, the athame is paired with a chalice to represent unity and the balance of opposites: masculine and feminine, action and receptivity, fire and water.

The Chalice

The chalice is a sacred cup used to hold water, wine, or other ritual liquids. It represents the element of water and is often associated with the feminine principle. In ritual, it can be used for offerings, blessings, or symbolic acts of union and fertility.

The chalice has ancient symbolism that appears in both magical and religious contexts. In Christianity, it is the central object in the Eucharist. In Celtic mythology, it is linked to the Holy Grail, a vessel of mystical transformation. In magical practice, drinking from the chalice can symbolize communion with divine forces, shared intent among participants, or the merging of inner and outer worlds.

The Pentacle

The pentacle is a flat disc inscribed with a five-pointed star, often made of wood, stone, or metal. It is often used in ritual by modern witches to represent the element of earth or the harmony of elements. The pentacle acts as a grounding tool and is chosen by some to charge, bless, or consecrate objects. For others, it acts simply as a nice piece of decor for an altar or sacred space.

The five points of the star are usually interpreted as the five elements: earth, air, fire, water, and spirit. The circle that surrounds them symbolizes unity, protection, and the cyclical nature of existence. Historically, the pentacle has been a symbol of health, protection, and sacred geometry long before its modern associations with witchcraft. It remains one of the most recognized, albeit misunderstood, symbols in magical practice today.

The Cauldron

The cauldron is a symbol of transformation, mystery, and rebirth. It represents the womb of the goddess, where ingredients come together to form something new. Traditionally associated with the element of water, the cauldron can also be linked to fire when used for burning herbs, incense, or small fires in ritual.

Cauldrons have a deep mythological presence, especially in Celtic lore. The Cauldron of Cerridwen was said to grant knowledge and inspiration. In modern witchcraft, cauldrons are often used to mix potions, burn petitions, or perform scrying by filling them with water and gazing into the surface. They can also serve as powerful symbols of death and rebirth, burning away negative energy and traumas in your life.

The Bell

The bell is used in ritual to mark transitions, call spirits, or cleanse energy. Its sound creates vibration that breaks up stagnant or negative forces in the space around you. Bells are often used to open and close sacred space, signal the beginning of a ritual, or call attention during trance or meditation. The clear tone of a bell helps shift awareness from the mundane to the sacred. In many cultures, from Buddhist temples to Catholic churches, bells have served as tools of spiritual invocation and purification. Some practitioners use different bells for different purposes, depending on their tone and material.

The Besom

The besom is a traditional witch's broom, symbolizing cleansing, protection, and preparation. Before a ritual, it may be swept around the ritual space to symbolically clear away stagnant energy. It is not used to clean physical dirt, but rather to purify the space energetically. Historically, the image of the broom is deeply linked with witches, often misunderstood through folklore. In reality, the besom is a powerful boundary-setting tool. It may be placed near the doorway for spiritual protection or used to ritually "sweep away" unwanted energies before or after magical work.

Crystals

While not always considered a tool in the traditional sense, crystals are widely used in modern magical practice for their unique energetic properties. Each stone is believed to hold distinct vibrations that can aid in healing, grounding, protection, manifestation, or spiritual awakening. Clear quartz is often used for amplification, rose quartz for love, obsidian for protection, and amethyst for spiritual insight. These are just a few of the thousands of crystals that exist with unique properties to uncover. In magical practice, they can be charged, placed on altars, carried in charms, or used in marking circles around sacred spaces.

Crystals are often said to vibrate at stable, consistent frequencies due to their precise internal structures. This stability is what makes them useful in both metaphysical and technological contexts. Quartz, for example, is used in watches and electronics to regulate time and energy. In magical practice, these steady vibrations are believed to interact with the human energy field, helping to realign imbalances and raise your internal frequency. By working with crystals, you can align your personal energy with the natural frequency of any stone, taking on its properties to amplify your rituals.

Herbs

Herbs are plants known for their medicinal, energetic, or symbolic properties, and they are used in magical practice for a wide range of purposes. In traditional witchcraft, herbs may be dried and stored in jars, bundled into charms or sachets, brewed into teas, or sprinkled around sacred areas. They are also used to dress candles, prepare ritual oils, or fill poppets and spell bags.

Each herb is said to have its own spiritual qualities. Sage is often chosen for cleansing and protection. Lavender supports peace and restfulness. Rosemary aids memory and mental clarity. Mugwort is associated with dreams and divination. Bay leaves are burned or written on for wish-making and manifestation. Many herbs are also linked to planets, zodiac signs, or deities, which adds layers of meaning to their use in magical work.

Beyond their symbolic roles, herbs are selected for their natural properties as well. Some cool and soothe, while others heat and stimulate. Their aroma, taste, and effect influence how they are used in spellcraft. For example, calming herbs might be included in a spell for emotional healing, while energizing herbs might be used in love or success magic. It's ultimately up to you to study their effects and decide which makes sense to use in your practice.

When herbs are used with intention, the spirit of the plant is invited into the ritual to work alongside you. Over time, some practitioners even form relationships with certain herbs, treating them as living allies rather than materials. Whether they are burned, steeped, scattered, or blended into charm bags, herbs help bring the power of the natural world into your practice.

Incense

Incense has been used in spiritual traditions around the world for thousands of years, from ancient Egyptian temples to Catholic cathedrals and Buddhist shrines. In magical practice, incense serves as a ritual tool that purifies space, shifts energy, and elevates consciousness. The rising smoke is believed to act as a bridge between the physical and spiritual realms, carrying prayers, intentions, and offerings to higher planes.

Each type of incense carries its own energetic signature. Frankincense is used for protection and spiritual elevation. Myrrh supports grounding and ancestral connection. Sandalwood encourages meditation and inner peace. Copal is often chosen for purification and sacred rites. When burned during ritual, incense can cleanse a room, set the tone for spellwork, and align the space with the desired elemental energy. In witchcraft, incense is most commonly linked with the element of air, often used for calling in other elemental spirits or to enhance intuition.

There are many forms of incense to choose from, including sticks, cones, resins, and loose herbal blends. Resin incense, such as frankincense or dragon's blood, is often placed on charcoal tablets in a cauldron for a more traditional experience. Loose blends allow for full customization and can be crafted to match specific magical workings. Stick incense allows for a quick and easy setup, requiring just a few moments under a lighter to begin working. However it is used, incense helps signal that a sacred space has been created and helps raise the intensity of your magic.

Candles

Candles represent the element of fire and the presence of divine light. They are used to illuminate sacred space, mark intentions, and focus willpower. The act of lighting a candle is one of the most accessible forms of magic. It is simple, but symbolic. A single flame can serve as a beacon for hope, clarity, transformation, and spiritual focus. In many traditions, the candle is treated as a living presence. Practitioners may speak to the flame, meditate in its glow, or visualize their desires being carried upward with the smoke and light.

The color of the candle is often chosen to match the purpose of your spellwork. Green is used for prosperity, growth, and abundance. Red ignites passion, vitality, and courage. White represents purity, clarity, or spiritual connection. Black is used for banishing, protection, and shadow work. Blue supports healing and communication. Purple is associated with psychic ability and power. Yellow enhances creativity and confidence. Choosing the right color helps tune the energy of the spell to its intended outcome.

Many witches further prepare their candles before use by anointing them with oils that align with their purpose. This is often done by rubbing oil onto the candle from the center outward, or from bottom to top, depending on whether the spell is meant to draw something in or release something away. Herbs may also be sprinkled onto the oiled surface or placed around the candle base. These herbs reinforce the spell's intention, connecting the work to the natural world.

Symbols, sigils, or runes may be carved or etched into the candle's wax using a pin, knife, or other ritual tool. These markings can act as magical signatures, embedding your intent directly into the candle. As the candle burns, it releases that intention into the world.

Candle magic can be as brief or elaborate as needed. Some may involve re-lighting the candle at each trip to your altar, while others are left to burn down in a single session. That being said, always ensure your safety is top priority when using fire in your practice, and never burn a candle in a space where it is clearly not safe to do so.

11

THE ALTAR

An altar is a dedicated space where spiritual or magical work takes place. It is often used as a surface for placing meaningful objects, performing rituals, or focusing intention. For some, it is a quiet place for prayer or reflection. For others, it is a working station for spells, divination, or honoring deities and ancestors. While the word "altar" may conjure images of churches or temples, personal altars can be found in bedrooms, gardens, kitchens, or even backpacks. What makes an altar sacred is not its location or appearance, but the intention behind it. It is any space that helps invite vulnerable connections with the self, the spirit, and the unseen forces of the world.

Historically, altars have been central to nearly every spiritual system in the world. In ancient Egypt, priests performed elaborate daily rituals at temple altars to feed and clothe the statues of the gods, believing these acts maintained cosmic order. In Greece and Rome, public and household altars were used to offer libations, burn incense, and make sacrifices in exchange for divine favor. In Hindu homes, family shrines still serve as daily meeting places between humans and the divine, with statues of deities lovingly bathed, dressed, and offered food and flowers.

Altars have also been present in monotheistic traditions. In Christianity, the church altar is a sacred space where communion is performed, symbolizing the presence of Christ and the renewal of spiritual covenant. In Judaism, the altar once stood at the center of the Temple in Jerusalem, where offerings were made to God as acts of devotion and repentance. Even in Islam, while altars as physical constructs are less prominent, the practice of facing Mecca during prayer transforms any space into a temporary sacred site.

In magical traditions, the altar functions both as a working space and as a spiritual anchor. It is the stage upon which rituals are performed, the place where tools are arranged, intentions are set, and offerings are made. It becomes a container of energy, holding your focus, intention, and relationship to the forces you work with. Whether you are casting a spell, honoring ancestors, or simply meditating, the altar acts as a gateway, allowing your actions to move beyond the mundane and into the spiritual.

Setting up your sacred space can be as simple or as elaborate as you wish. Some practitioners dedicate entire rooms to their spiritual practice, while others use a small shelf, a windowsill, or the top of a dresser. What matters is not the size of the space, but the sincerity of the intention behind it. When you create an altar, you are making a statement to yourself and the universe that this place is sacred. You are reminded that you are here with purpose.

The items placed on an altar often reflect the spiritual path of the practitioner. A Wiccan altar, for example, might include representations of the elements (earth, air, fire, and water) along with symbols of the Goddess and God. Candles, incense, crystals, a chalice, an athame, and a pentacle are commonly arranged with care and symmetry. Other traditions may place ancestral photos, sacred texts, statues of deities, animal bones, plants, or natural objects found during a walk in the woods. Every item has meaning and is chosen with intention, acting as a point of focus or a vessel for energy. If you practice paganism, you may even choose to dedicate an entire altar to just one deity, perhaps in an effort to gain their favor or draw upon their power.

Many altars change with the seasons. Practitioners who follow the Wheel of the Year often decorate their space with colors, symbols, and offerings that reflect the current seasonal festival. At Samhain, the altar might be adorned with autumn leaves, candles for the dead, and objects that represent the thinning of the veil. During Ostara, it might include spring flowers, eggs, and symbols of renewal. This seasonal rhythm helps practitioners stay connected to the cycles of nature and the flow of life.

There is no single correct way to use an altar. Some people begin each day by lighting a candle and sitting quietly at their altar, using the space to ground themselves or set intentions. Others visit it only during rituals or spiritual milestones. Some altars are private and used for personal reflection, while others are communal, inviting group rituals and shared energy. The altar may serve as a place of gratitude, a site for spellcasting, a memorial to ancestors, or simply a space where the practitioner feels most at peace.

Cleansing and maintaining the altar is considered important by many. Dusting it regularly, refreshing offerings, or smudging the area with herbs like sage or lavender helps keep the space energetically clear. Beyond keeping your space tidy, it is a way of showing respect to the spiritual forces you are inviting into your life. Just as you would not invite a guest into a neglected room, it is important to tend to your altar with care and presence.

Over time, an altar can begin to hold a kind of residual power. The more you work with it, the more it becomes a charged space that responds to your energy. Many practitioners report feeling a noticeable shift in consciousness when they sit at their altar, as if entering a quiet dialogue with the sacred. This is the power of consistency and ritual. The altar becomes not only a place to perform magic, but a place that feels magical in itself.

Ultimately, your altar is yours. It can reflect your beliefs, your culture, your history, and your hopes. It can be minimalist or overflowing, solemn or joyful, static or ever-changing. It is a canvas upon which your spiritual path can be expressed and explored. There is no hierarchy of worth when it comes to altars. A matchbox altar tucked in a backpack can be just as sacred as a lavish shrine adorned with gold and gemstones.

In creating an altar, you are not just building a space, but making a commitment to your practice. You are choosing to pause, to listen, and to make meaning out of the ordinary. Whether you are seeking spiritual guidance, offering thanks, or simply holding space for the sacred in your life, the altar remains one of the most timeless and personal tools for developing your spirituality.

12

THE ELEMENTS

L ong before modern science explained the building blocks of matter, ancient mystics and philosophers turned to the elements (earth, air, fire, and water) to make sense of the world. Elemental magic arose from this search for understanding, blending spiritual insight with the rhythms of nature. From Greece to India to China, mystics identified recurring forces that shaped existence: solid earth, flowing water, flickering fire, and invisible air. These elements were not just physical substances, but sacred principles that explained the balance of life and the nature of the soul.

In ancient Greece, the philosopher Empedocles first proposed the idea that all matter was composed of four root elements: earth, air, fire, and water. Plato later expanded on this idea, linking each element to a sacred geometric shape. Aristotle developed it further, describing the elements as fundamental building blocks that combined in various ways to form all matter. These ideas were not just limited to theory, as they influenced how people approached healing, agriculture, weather, emotions, and spiritual practice for centuries.

In India, the concept of the elements appears in the Ayurvedic and yogic traditions, where they are known as the Pancha Mahabhutas. These five great elements (earth, water, fire, air, and ether) are believed to compose the physical world and the human body. Each element corresponds to a different sense and bodily function, making them central not only to spiritual practice but also to medicine and daily living.

In traditional Chinese philosophy, a similar but distinct system known as the Wu Xing or Five Phases (wood, fire, earth, metal, and water) was developed. Though different in structure, this system also describes the cycles of nature and how energy moves through the world. It has been deeply influential in Chinese medicine, martial arts, astrology, and ritual magic.

Across indigenous cultures, elements were not theoretical concepts but living beings. Spirits of earth, fire, water, and air were honored, negotiated with, and relied upon. In animist traditions, the wind had a voice, the flame had a will, and water could remember. These forces were not just symbolic, but actual living entities. Elemental magic, in this older sense, was not about control over the elements, but about relationship with them.

Over time, these systems evolved and blended with one another. In the Western esoteric tradition, especially during the Renaissance, elemental theory was absorbed into the practice of alchemy, ceremonial magic, and the writings of mystics like Paracelsus. The four elements became cornerstones of magical correspondences, used to classify everything from herbs and stones to planets and spirits. By the time modern witchcraft and Wicca emerged in the twentieth century, elemental magic had already become a foundational part of most Western magical practice.

Each element is believed to have its own traits, temperament, and area of influence. They can be worked with individually or in balance. Some traditions also recognize a fifth element, often called spirit or aether, which represents the unifying force that binds the other four together. Others see spirit not as a separate element, but as the thread that runs through all creation. Regardless of the system you choose, the elements can serve as powerful allies in magical and spiritual work.

Earth is the element of stability, structure, and physical reality. It governs the material world: your home, your body, your health, your finances. It is associated with stones, soil, bones, and all things that endure. Earth energy is grounding. It helps you feel secure, focused, and connected to the present moment. In magic, it can be used for protection, manifestation, and long-term goals. Earth invites patience and reminds you that all things grow with time. It speaks through silence, weight, and stillness.

Air is the element of thought, intellect, and communication. It governs your mind, your breath, and your ability to express yourself. Air is light and ever-moving. It stirs ideas, opens doors, and carries your intentions across distance. Associated with wind, feathers, incense, and the sky, air magic helps with clarity, inspiration, and learning. It brings messages, both internal and external, and encourages freedom, perspective, and new beginnings. When you need to speak truth, learn something new, or let go of limiting beliefs, call on the energy of air.

Fire is the element of transformation, passion, and willpower. It governs your drive, your ambition, and your courage. Fire is energy in its most active form. It consumes, purifies, and renews. In magic, fire is used for empowerment, release, and dramatic change. It burns away what is no longer needed and ignites what is ready to rise. Fire is found in candles, the sun, lightning, and the spark in your own chest when you are inspired. It can be dangerous when uncontrolled, but sacred when respected. To work with fire is to invite movement, confidence, and the courage to take risks.

Water is the element of emotion, intuition, and healing. It governs the heart, the subconscious, and the cycles of life. Water flows through rivers and oceans, through tears and blood. It dissolves, nourishes, and remembers. In magical practice, water is used for purification, emotional balance, and connecting with the unseen. It helps you tune into your feelings and listen to your inner voice. Associated with cups, seashells, the moon, and dreams, water teaches you how to move with grace and respond with compassion. It speaks through emotion, rhythm, and reflection.

These four elements are not confined to nature. They live within you. Your body is made of earth. Your breath is air. Your digestion and energy are fire. Your blood and tears are water. Elemental magic recognizes that you are not separate from the world around you, but an expression of it. By working with these forces intentionally, you begin to harmonize with the natural rhythms of life. You stop resisting change and start flowing with it.

In ritual, elemental magic is often represented by placing objects for each element at the four directions. Earth is placed in the north, air in the east, fire in the south, and water in the west. These placements vary slightly across traditions, but the symbolism remains the same. Each direction becomes a gateway through which you can call upon that element's energy. Some practitioners also cast a circle, calling each element into the space to create a balanced and protected area for magical work.

You do not need to follow strict rules to begin working with elemental magic. You only need to become aware. Spend time in nature and notice how the elements speak to you. Sit on the ground and feel the pull of the earth beneath you. Listen to the wind and how it moves through the trees. Watch the flames of a fire or the flicker of a candle. Let yourself be lulled by the sound of rain or the flow of a stream. These are the voices of the elements, and they are always speaking.

You can also work with the elements in daily life. Cooking engages all four. Gardening connects you to earth and water. Singing and deep breathing invoke air. Dancing and exercise stir fire. Washing your hands, taking a bath, lighting incense, cleaning your space—all of these are small rituals that can become magical when done with intention. Even journaling or creative writing can become elemental magic when you let thoughts flow like air, express emotion like water, channel inspiration like fire, or ground ideas with the patience of earth.

Over time, you may find that you resonate more strongly with one element than the others. This can reflect your natural disposition or point to areas where growth is needed. Someone drawn to water may be deeply intuitive but struggle with boundaries. A fire-dominant person might be full of energy but easily burned out. Elemental balance is not about suppressing traits, but learning to integrate them. You are not trying to master the elements; you are building a relationship with them. Like any relationship, it requires respect, listening, and reciprocity.

Elemental magic can be practiced on its own or woven into any spiritual path. Wiccans often use the elements in casting circles and aligning with the seasons. Ceremonial magicians may assign planetary or astrological correspondences to each. Animists see the elements as living spirits. Chaos magicians use them symbolically to organize energy. However you choose to approach it, elemental magic is a flexible and powerful system that can be tailored to your own path.

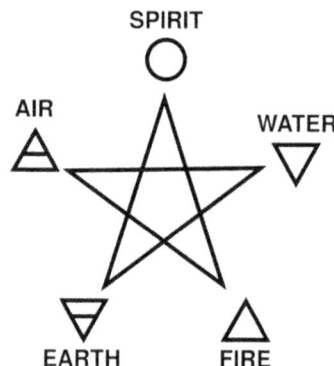

13

NATURE MAGIC

N ature magic is the practice of forming an intimate relationship with the living world and drawing upon its power to exact change. It begins with listening to the wind in the trees, the shift of seasons, and the quiet presence of spirit in every part of the landscape. In this worldview, the earth is not a backdrop, but a sacred being. Mountains, rivers, forests, and animals are seen as holders of wisdom. Magic arises not through separation from the world, but through deeper participation in it.

Many ancient spiritual systems reflect this deep respect for the land, including the animist beliefs of indigenous peoples and the nature-centric traditions of pre-Christian Europe. Celtic Druidry embodied this reverence for nature in its purest form. Sacred groves, stones, and trees were central to the Celtic understanding of spirit. Their year revolved around the land's cycles. Their stories spoke of gods who walked the earth and lived in the hills. Their magic was not an escape from the world, but a way of becoming more deeply embedded within it. This connection to the natural world continues in the practices of modern nature-based witches, especially those who walk the path of the green witch.

A green witch is someone whose magic is rooted in the plant

kingdom. They work closely with herbs, trees, flowers, roots, and fungi, forming relationships with the land and its cycles. These witches are often gardeners, foragers, herbalists, or kitchen witches, but green witchcraft goes beyond using plants for practical purposes. It is about recognizing plants as teachers and allies. A green witch learns to classify herbs based on their effects, while also understanding that each plant has a unique presence, personality, and spirit.

Nature magic as a whole is built on the principle of reciprocity. A green witch may sing to their plants, harvest with care, or leave offerings in the soil. They pay attention to when a plant wants to be picked and when it should be left alone. The process of planting, tending, and gathering becomes ritual in itself. Magic flows through the garden, the kitchen, the apothecary shelf, and the forest floor.

Many herbs are thought to hold magical significance, either due to real physical properties or from stories passed down through generations. By utilizing herbs in spellwork, you can turn even the simplest acts into something magical. Brewing tea becomes a healing spell when made with lavender and intention. Placing bay leaves beneath your pillow becomes a tool for dreamwork. Lighting a candle dressed with cinnamon becomes a charm for success. The possibilities truly are endless. Below are just a few examples of how you can utilize some common herbs to elevate you practice.

Lavender: Used for peace, sleep, and emotional healing. Its scent is calming and protective, perfect for cleansing energy or aiding rest.

Rosemary: A powerful herb of memory, clarity, and purification. Burned to clear a space or placed at the door for protection.

Mugwort: A lunar herb that enhances dreams and psychic work. Used in teas, incense, or sleep sachets to open the inner eye.

Basil: Draws love, abundance, and joy. Grown by the door or carried in charms to invite good fortune.

Yarrow: Strengthens boundaries and offers protection. Used for courage in difficult emotional situations.

Mint: Energizing and refreshing. Supports focus, confidence, and renewal.

Dandelion: A resilient and magical plant for wishes, divination, and spirit communication.

Most green witches keep a notebook filled with herbal notes, seasonal wisdom, recipes, and spellwork. They may dry herbs for bundles, press flowers into journals, or infuse oils with blossoms gathered under the moon. An at-home apothecary might hold teas, salves, tinctures, incense, and sacred waters. Over time, a green witch comes to know which plant to call upon for each type of magic, whether for protection, love, healing, release, or manifestation.

Some green witches also engage in plant spirit communication, connecting with a plant's essence through meditation or dreamwork. These moments are quiet, intuitive, and personal. They allow the witch to understand not just what a plant does, but what it feels like. Nettle may teach how to defend without closing off. Violet may offer comfort during grief. These are teachings that cannot be memorized from books, only learned through experience.

Since nature magic follows the rhythms of the natural world, many green witches align their work with the Wheel of the Year, marking seasonal shifts with planting, harvesting, or resting. Lunar phases may also guide their practice, using new moons for sowing intentions, full moons for empowerment, and waning moons for letting go. Gardening becomes a ceremony. Cooking becomes alchemy. Everyday life becomes a ritual!

What sets green witchcraft apart from other systems of magic is its groundedness. It does not rely on formal initiations or expensive tools. A sprig of thyme, a mason jar, and a walk through the woods is more than enough. Despite its name, you do not need to live in the countryside to begin this path. A few herbs on a windowsill, a walk through a city park, or a cup of herbal tea shared in silence can open the way for you, even if you live in a bustling metropolis. What matters is your intention and reverence for nature. To practice nature magic is to treat the world as sacred and to live in quiet collaboration with the life around you.

14

KITCHEN MAGIC

Kitchen magic, sometimes known as hearth magic or cottage witchcraft, is a practical way to turn everyday cooking into spellwork. It is built on the idea that the home, especially the kitchen, is a sacred space where transformation takes place. The kitchen is where raw ingredients become nourishment, herbs become medicine, and intention becomes manifestation. To work magic in the kitchen is to infuse everyday tasks with spiritual meaning. It is where the physical and the magical come together in the most accessible and embodied way.

At the heart of kitchen magic is the belief that intention can elicit real change. The act of preparing a meal becomes sacred when it is done with love, gratitude, and presence. Stirring a soup while thinking about protection, sprinkling cinnamon on oatmeal while visualizing abundance, or baking bread with the hope of bringing people together are all acts of spellwork. By consuming food and drink that has been infused with intentions, you allow it to disperse throughout your body and become a part of you. It can be a powerful and vulnerable way to create change in your life.

One of the best parts of kitchen magic is its accessibility to so many people. If you have a working kitchen, then you are basically ready to go! A mortar and pestle may be used to grind herbs and seeds. Wooden spoons can stir energy and set intentions while preparing food. Glass jars and bottles are great for storing ingredients like oils, tinctures, and dried herbs. A kitchen knife used for carving symbols into ingredients can act as a ritual athame. Even simple pots and pans can be reimagined as cauldrons for brewing potions.

These tools do not need to be set aside from your normal kitchen equipment. What matters is how you use them. Magic lives in ordinary things that are used with purpose.

Potions

Potions are one of the most recognizable forms of kitchen magic, although the process of brewing a potion is often much simpler than popular stories would suggest. A potion does not need to bubble in a cauldron or glow with mystical light. It can be as humble as a cup of tea brewed with intention, a broth simmered with healing herbs, or a syrup stirred slowly while whispering a prayer.

Potions are liquid spells crafted to bring about change, healing, clarity, or connection. They rely on the magical and medicinal properties of herbs, spices, and natural ingredients brought together through ritual and purpose. Each method has a different effect depending on the ingredients and the goal of the spell. Below are some of the common types of potions you may encounter when exploring kitchen magic.

Teas are simple infusions made by steeping herbs in hot water. They are one of the most accessible and effective forms of potion.

Tinctures are created by steeping herbs in alcohol for several weeks. They are concentrated and used in small doses for healing or energy work.

Syrups are made by combining herbal infusions with honey or sugar.

They are often used for throat soothing or to sweeten a magical drink.

Vinegars, also called oxymels when mixed with honey, are made by soaking herbs in apple cider vinegar. They can be used both magically and medicinally.

Elixirs are more ceremonial blends that often combine herbs, natural sweeteners, and symbolic elements. They are usually consumed in small ritual amounts.

The combination of herbs you select will dictate the outcome of your brew based on their magical effects. A tea of rose petals, hibiscus, and cinnamon stirred with honey becomes a love potion that opens the heart to romance or self-love. Peppermint, rosemary, and lemon balm brewed together form a clarity potion that clears the mind and strengthens focus. Ginger, garlic, and cayenne steeped in apple cider vinegar create a protection tonic that strengthens boundaries and immunity. Chamomile and mugwort brewed together make a dream potion to enhance sleep and spiritual visions. These are just a few of the countless combinations you can explore for yourself when brewing potions.

Most importantly, you must always research the herbs you use to ensure they are safe to touch or consume. Some magical herbs are toxic if ingested or only safe in very small amounts. Part of the path of a kitchen witch is knowing the difference and using your ingredients responsibly. Remember that potions do not *have* to be imbibed to work. They can be anointed on your skin, added to baths, used to cleanse objects, or simply displayed on a shelf.

Cooking as Spellwork

In the hands of a mindful kitchen witch, cooking itself can be considered an act of magic. When you choose ingredients that correspond to your goal and prepare them with focused intention, you are essentially casting a spell.

Imagine you are attempting to bake some bread as a spell for abundance. As you knead the dough, you focus on what you want to grow in your life. You might even carve a symbol into the crust before baking and recite a small prayer to your chosen deity as you carry it into the oven. When eaten, this now sacred bread disperses intentions of abundance throughout your body, aligning your unconscious mind with the outcome of your spell. By focusing intently on abundance, you will find that opportunities begin to open up for you where you had never even thought to look.

Similarly, making a soup can act as a spell for healing. You can choose herbs that have comforting or immune-boosting qualities, and stir the pot with a wooden spoon while imagining any pain leaving the body. If you suffer from chronic gastrointestinal issues that are outside of the scope of western doctors, cooking intentionally can be a great way to help physically soothe your body while also spiritually aligning the soul.

You can even use seasonings as part of your spellwork. Salt is often used for protection, while pepper banishes negativity. You can write wishes on bay leaves and add them to your dish or whisper affirmations over your spices before adding them to your food. When making sweet treats, use uplifting herbs like lemon balm or vanilla to elicit feelings of lightheartedness and pleasure in your guests. For savory dishes, basil can bring prosperity and abundance to your meals. As a kitchen witch, you will have to find what seasonings work best for you and your practice.

Many kitchen witches also align their work with the cycles of nature. Seasonal cooking and lunar timing add an extra layer of power to your meals and potions. You might harvest herbs at the full moon to charge them with clarity and light. You might brew a tonic at the new moon to support fresh beginnings. You might bake at the solstice using seasonal fruits and sacred grains. Following the Wheel of the Year can help you root your practice in nature's rhythm and has many overlaps with nature magic.

If you live in a space where you cannot practice magic openly, you can still turn daily meals into quiet rituals. Lighting a candle before you cook, giving thanks before you eat, or placing a flower on the counter as a small altar helps keep your space sacred. Kitchen magic is a practice that truly does blend seamlessly with everyday life. You do not need formal training, a special background, or rare tools. Stirring tea with love, cooking a meal for someone who is grieving, or crafting herbal honey for the changing seasons are all honest expressions of this gentle and powerful path.

In many ways, you are already performing magic every time you cook with love or share food with intention. Food is such an integral part of human society, so why not include it in your spiritual practice? With kitchen magic, the altar is your cutting board, the cauldron is your pot, and the ritual is your recipe. Now that you are aware of this power, you can turn even the most simple of tasks into everyday acts of magic.

15

SIGILS & SYMBOLIC MAGIC

Sigil magic is the practice of turning intention into symbol. It is one of the most accessible and creative forms of magic, requiring no elaborate tools or rituals. Practitioners are able to shape desire into a visual form that speaks directly to your unconscious mind. Through a process of creation, focus, and release, a sigil becomes a vessel for willpower and transformation.

A sigil is a symbol crafted from a specific intention. It does not represent a broad concept like love or protection but a focused desire, such as "*I am safe in my home*" or "*my work is seen and valued.*" By translating these statements into an abstract design, the conscious mind steps aside and allows the deeper self to carry the desire into action. This symbolic form bypasses doubt, fear, and overthinking. It slips past the filters of logic and enters the more mysterious layers of awareness where change often begins.

The origins of symbolic magic stretch back to ancient times. Sacred symbols have been used in nearly every culture to represent power, healing, protection, and spiritual truths. Runes, hieroglyphs, veves, and magical alphabets all served as early forms of symbolic language. But the modern method of sigil creation is often credited to the artist and occultist Austin Osman Spare. He taught that desire must be focused and then forgotten. He saw the unconscious as a fertile field where the seeds of will could grow, but only if left undisturbed by doubt or overanalysis.

Creating a sigil is both an act of magic and art. It begins with a statement of intention, written clearly and in the present tense. The statement should be simple, personal, and affirming. Take the statement below as an example:

I attract peaceful relationships.
I heal with strength and patience.
I open new paths for my creativity.

Once the statement is chosen, you remove all repeating letters. What remains are the core letters of the phrase. These letters are then rearranged, overlapped, or stylized into a unique symbol. The final design should be abstract, not easily connected to the original sentence. It can be as simple or complex as you like. Curves, lines, dots, and angles can all be used to create a balanced shape that feels complete and resonant.

The act of drawing a sigil is part of the spell. Focus your energy as you draw it. Let your mind grow quiet. Let your body settle into a rhythm. Some people redraw the sigil several times until it feels right. Others use one version and carry it with them. There is no single correct way. The power comes from your intention and your connection to the process.

Once the sigil is created, it must be charged. Charging means filling it with emotional, mental, or physical energy. This can be done through meditation, chanting, dancing, visualization, breathwork, or even moments of intense emotion. The goal is to build a surge of focused energy while holding the sigil in your mind or gaze. When the moment peaks, you let the energy pass into the symbol.

After charging, the final step is release. This means letting go of your attachment to the outcome. You may choose to burn the sigil, bury it, hide it, or simply forget its meaning. The idea is to send the desire into the world without clinging to it. Obsession with change blocks the natural flow of magic. Letting go creates space for change to unfold on its own.

Sigils are not limited to ritual spaces, they can be used just about anywhere. Some are drawn on paper and tucked into wallets or journals. Others are carved into candles, traced on skin, or blended into artwork. You can place one under your pillow for dreamwork, draw one on a mirror for confidence, or hide one in a garden to nurture growth. Some people create sigils for long-term goals while others make quick, daily sigils for focus and clarity. The method is flexible. What matters is the meaning you give it.

One powerful aspect of sigil magic is its privacy. Unlike spells that require words or objects, a sigil can be kept completely secret. No one else needs to know what it means. This makes it especially useful for quiet, personal work. It can be carried in a notebook, worn as jewelry, or included in a painting without drawing attention. If burned in a cauldron, nobody will *ever* see it. The magic is yours alone.

Over time, you may find that your sigils become more intuitive. You might begin to sketch symbols without a formal process and recognize their meaning later. You might dream of a shape and wake up already knowing its significance. This is part of the deepening relationship with your unconscious. Sigil magic opens a door to your inner world and invites it to speak back to you.

It is important to remember that sigils are not about forcing the world to obey your will. They are about aligning your energy with an intention and creating space for that change to occur. They are subtle, symbolic, and personal. A sigil is a reminder that magic begins with clarity, is fueled by intention, and is fulfilled through trust. With just a pen and a piece of paper, you hold the power to reshape the story you are living!

16

ASTROLOGY

A strology is the study of how the positions of the stars and planets influence human life and spiritual energy. Long before it became associated with newspaper horoscopes or pop culture memes, it was a sacred science that sought to understand the relationship between the heavens and the soul. Practiced by ancient cultures across Babylon, Egypt, Greece, India, and China, astrology was used not only to predict events but to understand divine will, human personality, and the cycles of fate that govern life on earth.

At its heart, astrology is the belief that the positions and movements of celestial bodies reflect deeper truths about our lives. The stars are not just distant points of light. They are mirrors of the soul. The planets are not just rocks in orbit. They are symbols of archetypal forces that shape human experience. When you were born, the sky was arranged in a unique pattern that many believe reveals your personality, your challenges, your gifts, and even your spiritual purpose.

The birth chart, also known as the natal chart, is a map of the sky at the exact moment and place of your birth. It shows the position of the sun, moon, and planets in the twelve signs of the zodiac and the twelve houses of life. Each of these elements represents a layer of who you are and how you relate to the world. The sun reflects your core identity. The moon shows your emotions and inner self. Mercury governs your mind and communication. Venus rules love and attraction. Mars represents willpower and drive. Jupiter brings growth and expansion. Saturn teaches responsibility and limits. Uranus sparks change and rebellion. Neptune reveals dreams and illusions. Pluto confronts power and transformation.

The zodiac signs are not just personality types. They are symbolic expressions of energy. Aries is bold and initiating. Taurus is grounded and sensual. Gemini is curious and verbal. Cancer is nurturing and protective. Leo is radiant and expressive. Virgo is analytical and healing. Libra is balanced and relational. Scorpio is intense and transformative. Sagittarius is expansive and philosophical. Capricorn is structured and ambitious. Aquarius is visionary and unique. Pisces is intuitive and mystical. The sign a planet is in changes how that planet expresses itself, just as the tone of a voice changes the meaning of a word.

Astrology does not end with your birth chart. It is also a living system that tracks the movement of the planets over time. These movements, known as transits, reflect the energetic themes and challenges of a particular moment. When a planet in the sky forms a relationship to a planet in your chart, it can signal a time of growth, tension, change, or opportunity. By observing these cycles, many spiritual practitioners use astrology as a tool for timing their rituals, planning their intentions, and navigating life with more awareness.

Many forms of magic align themselves with planetary energy. For example, someone casting a spell for abundance may choose to do so on a Thursday, the day ruled by Jupiter. A spell for love might be best on a Friday, which is associated with Venus. These correspondences extend to the planetary hours as well, dividing each day into segments where the energy of a specific planet is most influential. This system allows practitioners to align their magic with cosmic rhythms, adding layers of potency and timing to their work.

Lunar magic is one of the most accessible forms of astrology. The phases of the moon offer a simple but powerful cycle to work with. The new moon is for planting seeds, setting intentions, and beginning new projects. The waxing moon builds energy and is ideal for attraction and growth. The full moon is a time of culmination, illumination, and release. The waning moon is for letting go, banishing, and inner work. Each full moon also falls under a zodiac sign, adding a flavor of energy to its effects. A full moon in Scorpio, for instance, might bring themes of emotional depth and transformation, while a full moon in Leo may heighten creativity and confidence.

Astrology is not about fate in the rigid sense. It does not say that you are doomed to suffer or destined to succeed. Instead, it offers a symbolic language for understanding the forces at play in your life. It helps you recognize patterns, choose the best times to act, and make peace with the things you cannot control. It invites you to learn from the cosmos rather than fight against them. Your birth chart is not a box. It is a mirror and a map that shows you where the rivers of your energy flow most freely.

There are many forms of astrology across different cultures. Western astrology focuses on the tropical zodiac and individual psychology. Vedic astrology from India, known as Jyotish, is more predictive and rooted in karma. Chinese astrology follows a twelve-year lunar cycle based on animal signs and elements. Each system has its wisdom, and you may find that one speaks to you more than the others. Exploring these traditions can help you discover which form of astrology best aligns with your worldview and goals.

To begin working with astrology, you do not need to know everything at once. Start with your sun, moon, and rising signs. These three placements form the backbone of your chart. Your sun is your essence. Your moon is your emotional world. Your rising sign, or ascendant, is the mask you wear and the way others first perceive you. As you grow more comfortable, you can explore the deeper layers of your chart. Look at the houses, the aspects, the nodes of the moon, and the placement of Chiron and other asteroids. Each piece can help tell a story about your spiritual self.

Astrology is both an art and a science. It requires intuition, study, and a willingness to explore the unknown. For some, it becomes a daily practice. For others, it is an occasional mirror to reflect on life's changes. There is no one way to use astrology. You might track the moon cycles in your journal, set new moon intentions, or observe your personal transits during difficult times. You might use your chart to understand relationships, choose career directions, or explore your shadow. However you choose to work with it, astrology can be a deeply validating and empowering tool for spiritual growth.

As with any spiritual system, approach astrology with humility and care. It can be a map, but not a rulebook. It can reveal patterns, but it cannot take away your agency. It is not meant to replace your intuition, but to support it. Use astrology as a companion on your journey; a conversation between you and the stars. Let it teach you the intersections of fate and choice to help you understand your unique place in the great story of life.

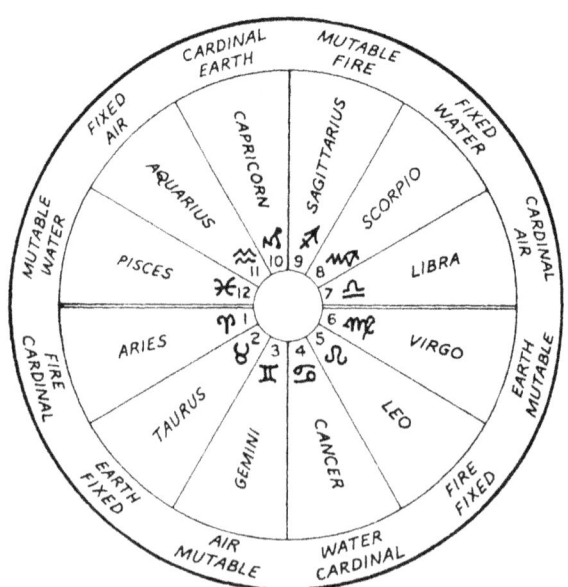

17

DIVINATION

Divination is the practice of seeking insight through signs, symbols, or patterns. For some, it is an attempt to look into the future or receive prophetic messages from unseen forces. The practice of divination likely developed as an extension of animism, as many early humans looked to nature for guidance and wisdom. They would read the cracks in bones, the behavior of birds, or the way leaves floated on water as divine messages warning of impending danger. In a time when any wrong move could result in your death, it's easy to see how divination may have naturally emerged as a way for early humans to feel better prepared for their uncertain future.

Across ancient cultures, divination served both practical and sacred purposes. It helped people decide when to plant crops, whether to go to war, whom to marry, or how to treat an illness. In many societies, it was considered a direct form of communication with the gods, the ancestors, or the spirit world. In ancient Greece, the Oracle of Delphi would enter states of trance to deliver prophecies from the god Apollo. In ancient Mesopotamia, trained diviners read omens in the stars and in the livers of sacrificed animals. In early China, bones were heated until they cracked, and the resulting lines were read like sacred maps. These practices were not taken lightly. Divination required discipline, observation, and often years of study. It was seen as a responsibility, not entertainment.

Though the tools have changed over time, the essence of divination remains the same. It is not about predicting the future with certainty, but about revealing patterns, offering perspective, and awakening your intuition. It invites you to pause and reflect to see what is often overlooked, and in doing so, connect with something larger than yourself. Divination is far deeper than just fortune telling. It is a tool for self-discovery, healing, and spiritual connection. It can help clarify a decision, unlock a feeling, or reveal the hidden energy within a situation.

The most common forms of divination today involve tarot cards, runes, pendulums, and astrology, but almost anything can be used when approached with the right intentions. A single candle flame can reveal truth if looked into long enough. A dream can offer prophecy when analyzed. The way a bird flies across the sky can carry a message meant just for you. Divination teaches you to pay attention and connect the dots when you can.

Tarot Cards

One of the most popular forms of modern divination is the use of tarot cards. Tarot has a long and layered history, with mundane origins that much later developed into a magical practice. The earliest known tarot decks appeared in 15th-century Italy as elaborate playing cards for a game called tarocchi. These early decks were commissioned by wealthy families and featured lavish illustrations with allegorical scenes. Over time, occultists began to see deeper symbolic meaning in the imagery, aligning the cards with mystical systems of alchemy, astrology, Kabbalah, and Hermeticism.

By the 18th and 19th centuries, tarot had been adopted into the Western magical tradition as a tool for spiritual insight. Occultists like Antoine Court de Gébelin and Éliphas Lévi helped reframe the tarot deck as a tool for accessing ancient wisdom, connecting it to

Egyptian mythology and esoteric symbolism. The most influential modern tarot deck, the *Rider-Waite-Smith Tarot*, was published in 1909 under the guidance of mystic Arthur Edward Waite and illustrated by artist Pamela Colman Smith. This deck, rich with symbolic detail, became the foundation for many contemporary interpretations and remains one of the most widely used decks today.

Tarot consists of a structured deck of seventy-eight cards, each with its own symbolism and story. These cards are divided into the major arcana, which represent large spiritual themes or life-changing events, and the minor arcana, which reflect daily experiences and emotional currents. Each card carries layers of meaning, but it is the reader's intuition that brings those meanings to life within the context of a question or situation.

The major arcana contains twenty-two cards, beginning with The Fool and ending with The World. These cards are often seen as the soul's journey through life, with each stage representing a key spiritual lesson or turning point. The appearance of a major arcana card in a reading suggests a moment of heightened significance, a crossroads, or a deep shift in awareness. Cards such as The Lovers, Death, or The Tower do not always indicate literal events, but rather internal transformations or major archetypal forces at work in your life.

The minor arcana is made up of fifty-six cards divided into four suits, traditionally wands, cups, swords, and pentacles, each corresponding to an element and a realm of experience. Wands are associated with fire and represent passion, creativity, and action. Cups align with water and govern emotion, intuition, and relationships. Swords correspond to air and deal with thought, communication, and conflict. Pentacles represent earth and speak to material concerns such as work, health, and stability. Each suit contains ten numbered cards (ace through ten) and four court cards (page, knight, queen, and king) which often represent people, energies, or evolving aspects of the self.

Contrary to what you might think, tarot reading is not about predicting a fixed future. Instead, it offers a mirror for your inner world, helping you to see what is present, what is possible, and what patterns are ready to shift. Some readings are done with simple one-card or three-card spreads, offering insight into a specific question or situation. Others use more elaborate layouts, such as the Celtic Cross, to explore deeper layers of influence and choice. You can even make your own spread that is entirely unique to your practice.

The true magic of tarot lies in its ability to speak through symbol and metaphor. Over time, many readers form personal relationships with their decks, learning to trust the subtle impressions, emotions, and imagery that arise during a reading. It is through this intuitive dialogue that tarot becomes an incredibly effective tool for self reflection.

Oracle Cards

Oracle cards are an alternative form of divination that offer flexible, accessible guidance without the structured system found in traditional tarot. Unlike tarot, which follows a specific format of seventy-eight cards divided into major and minor arcana, oracle decks can include any number of cards and are shaped entirely by the unique vision of the creator. This freedom allows oracle cards to explore other focused themes, like angels, animal spirits, goddesses, ancestors, elemental forces, or affirmations for healing and empowerment.

Each deck has its own symbolic language, and the messages are often designed to be direct, supportive, and easy to interpret. For this reason, oracle cards are popular with beginners and seasoned practitioners alike. Some use them as daily prompts for reflection, while others incorporate them into rituals, spellwork, or longer readings. A single card can provide insight into your emotional state, spiritual path, or the energy surrounding a specific question or decision.

While oracle cards do not rely on any fixed tradition, they still require an intuitive connection. The process of pulling a card, sitting with its image and message, and relating it to your current experience is what gives the reading its power. By paying attention to how a card and its message makes you feel, you are entering into a conversation with your inner wisdom to better understand how to make positive changes in your life.

Many practitioners keep multiple oracle decks on hand, choosing which one to work with based on the energy of the day or the kind of guidance they seek. Some blend oracle and tarot cards in the same reading to offer both structure and flow. Others treat oracle cards as gentle allies for emotional healing, creative inspiration, or spiritual encouragement. There is no right or wrong way to use cards in divination, so long as you are getting something meaningful out of them.

Pendulums

A pendulum is a small weight or crystal, suspended from a chain, thread, or cord. It is used to answer yes or no questions, locate energy imbalances, or gain insight into subtle situations. When held still by the practitioner, the pendulum begins to move in response to subtle shifts in energy, unconscious muscle movement, or what some interpret as spiritual or intuitive guidance. Though it may seem simple, it can be a thrilling experience to see your pendulum move on its own.

Pendulums typically respond through specific directional swings. For example, a back-and-forth motion might indicate yes, while a circular motion could mean no. Many practitioners begin by asking their pendulum to show them what each response looks like, creating a personal system of communication. With time and consistent practice, the pendulum can become a trusted tool for quick and effective guidance.

Some people use pendulum boards, charts, or maps to explore more detailed questions, such as dates, names, or locations. Others prefer to hold the pendulum over energy centers in the body to detect blockages and flow. The practice is highly intuitive and can be adapted to suit many styles of spiritual work.

Pendulums are often weighted with crystals, such as amethyst for clarity, rose quartz for emotional healing, or black tourmaline for grounding and protection. However, the material is less important than the relationship you develop with the tool. Even a small stone found in nature and tied with some string can serve as a perfectly fine pendulum. What matters most is using pendulums with clear intention and thoughtful questions.

Rune Casting

Rune casting is a form of divination and symbolic magic rooted in the ancient spiritual traditions of Northern Europe, particularly Norse and Germanic cultures. The word "rune" comes from an old Germanic root meaning "secret" or "whisper," as each rune carries a unique message tied to myth, nature, emotion, or life's challenges.

A typical rune set includes twenty-four symbols from the Elder Futhark, the oldest known runic alphabet. Some sets include a blank rune, sometimes called the "wyrd" or "void" rune, representing the unknowable or the hand of fate. The symbols are traditionally carved or painted onto small stones, pieces of wood, or bone, and then stored in a pouch or sacred container. When used in a reading, runes are drawn or cast onto a cloth, and their orientation, position, and relationship to one another are all taken into account during interpretation.

Each rune acts as a symbolic key to truths about your own life. For example, Fehu represents wealth and abundance, Ansuz speaks to communication and divine messages, Raidho relates to journeys and movement, and Hagalaz warns of disruption or necessary change. Some runes are gentle and nurturing, while others bring challenge, shadow, and transformation. Their meanings are not always literal, as they sometimes point to abstract internal states or larger spiritual currents.

Rune casting can be done in many ways. A single rune draw may offer clarity for a specific situation. A three-rune spread might reveal the past, present, and future or the influences, obstacles, and outcome related to a question. More elaborate casts, such as the nine-rune grid or the "rune wheel," explore complex issues or long-term energies. Some practitioners even scatter runes and read only the ones that land upright or within a certain boundary, allowing chance and fate to guide the message.

Unlike tarot, which offers narrative through illustrated scenes, rune casting is more abstract. The symbols demand a deeper intuitive engagement and often speak in riddles or archetypes. The messages can feel stark, poetic, and deeply ancestral, but are sometimes too complicated for novice diviners to interpret. Don't feel discouraged if you run into difficulty. Magic takes practice, and with enough time you will begin to piece together these abstract messages much faster.

Scrying

Scrying is an ancient form of divination that involves gazing into a reflective or translucent surface to receive visions, symbols, or impressions. It invites the mind to enter a receptive, trance-like state where intuition and inner sight can take over. The word "scry" comes from an old English term meaning "to reveal" or "to perceive dimly," which captures the essence of the practice.

Traditional tools for scrying include mirrors, bowls of water, polished stones, crystals, glass, fire, or even smoke. One of the most iconic forms is the black mirror, often made of obsidian and used to soften visual input, allowing images to arise naturally in the mind's eye. Others may scry using candle flames, watching the dance of fire to receive signs or omens. Water scrying is another method, where a still bowl of water is gazed into under moonlight or ritual lighting.

The process of scrying is meant to be personal and intuitive. There is no fixed system of meanings and no cards or symbols to memorize. Instead, the practitioner allows their awareness to drift as they focus gently on the surface before them. Over time, shapes may appear, thoughts may rise, or inner voices may whisper meaning. These impressions are not always literal. You may encounter symbolic fragments, often coming from the unconscious mind, that require contemplation and interpretation to understand.

Scrying is often used to gain insight into hidden truths, explore dreams, connect with spirit guides, or receive messages about the future. It can also serve as a form of meditation or ritual visioning. Before beginning, many practitioners cleanse their tools, establish a sacred space, and enter a calm, focused mindset. It helps to have a clear question or area of focus, but the practice also welcomes openness to whatever arises.

As with all forms of divination, trust and patience are essential. Scrying is not about forcing visions to appear, but about quieting the mind enough to allow what is already waiting to surface. With regular practice, the scryer develops a stronger connection to their intuitive senses and a greater ability to interpret symbols as they arise.

Astrology

Astrology is a complex and ancient form of divination that is rooted in the belief that the position of celestial bodies influences life on earth. Most notably, astrology divides humans into archetypes or "signs" that are thought to guide the decision making of people in predictable ways. Since we have already covered astrology in detail, we will not be discussing it here. You may refer to the previous chapter for more information.

THOUGH WE HAVE COVERED many established forms of divination, some practitioners choose a more personal or eclectic approach. You might pull a random page from a book to find a message. You might break a wishbone in half to answer a question. You might interpret your dreams each morning, keeping a journal to track recurring symbols. What matters most is not the tool, but the relationship you form with it. Divination is a conversation with unseen forces, and not a command. It requires openness, curiosity, and humility to work properly.

A common misconception is that divination is about control. In truth, it is about surrender. It asks you to trust what arises without forcing an answer. Sometimes the message is clear. Other times it reveals itself slowly, like mist clearing at dawn. A good reading does not always tell you what you want to hear. Instead, it shows you what you need to understand. It reflects the energy of the present and invites you to participate in the unfolding story of your life.

Divination is not reserved for special occasions. It can be part of daily life. You might pull a card each morning to set your focus. You might ask a question before meditation and wait for a sign in the day ahead. You might use it at turning points when you feel lost or overwhelmed. Over time, divination becomes less about seeking answers and more about deepening your connection with the unseen. It becomes a way of walking through the world with greater presence.

18

PROTECTION & WARDING

P rotection magic is the practice of using spiritual techniques to shield people or places from unwanted influence. It is the art of maintaining boundaries, clearing harmful energies, and creating a safe environment for the spirit to thrive. Throughout history, people have used charms, symbols, herbs, prayers, and rituals to ward off danger. These might be physical threats, emotional disturbances, spiritual attacks, or simply energies that do not belong in your space. From the evil eye amulets of the Mediterranean to protective salt lines in folk traditions, these practices speak to a deep human desire for security and clarity. Protection magic is personal and practical, helping you feel safe in your body and home!

Protection magic can also be a valuable tool to help you reclaim your power after experiences of trauma, manipulation, or fear. Rather than building walls, protection magic invites you to create conscious, flexible boundaries. These are not meant to isolate you, but to preserve your energy and allow true connection. Healthy protection allows you to move through the world with greater confidence, grounded in your center and clear in your purpose.

Protection magic is often used before and after rituals to prepare and close the sacred space. It is also common during periods of stress, grief, or change, when energy is more vulnerable to outside influence. Just as you might lock your door at night or wear sunscreen in the sun, protection magic becomes part of your spiritual hygiene.

There are countless ways to practice protection magic, many of which require nothing more than intention and attention. That being said, let's briefly explore some of the most common techniques.

Cleansing

Before any protective work can take hold, it is important to remove what does not belong. Cleansing is the process of clearing unwanted energy from a space, object, or person. This can be done with smoke from herbs (like rosemary or cedar), saltwater, sound, breath, or even visualization. Many Native American nations still use sage and palo santo as tools for spiritual cleansing, though these herbs are becoming endangered in recent years. A simple cleansing practice might involve sprinkling salt around a room, ringing a bell in each corner, or imagining a wave of white light washing over you.

Warding

Warding is the act of creating protective boundaries, either around your body, home, or sacred space. You might place protective runes on doors and windows, bury charged crystals in the four corners of your property, or imagine a sphere of light surrounding you. Wards can be renewed regularly or charged during specific moon phases or seasonal transitions. In fact, modern witches frequently use warding to cast a "circle of power" before important rituals, removing any negative energy from their ritual space. Elements like these can help raise the significance of your rituals, making them feel more powerful.

Talismans

A talisman is a protective object that has been created with intention through the act of ritual. To make one, begin with a clear purpose, such as guarding your energy or deflecting negativity. Choose a meaningful base item (a pendant, coin, pouch, carved wood, or drawn symbol) then cleanse it with smoke, water, salt, or sound. Speak your intention aloud as you work, charging the object with your will. You can add symbols, thread, herbs, or oil to strengthen its purpose. Once complete, carry it, wear it, or place it somewhere sacred to let it serve as a physical anchor for your protective magic.

Symbols, Runes, and Sigils

Symbols represent visualized intent and carry great power. You can draw protective runes or sigils on doors, mirrors, or your own skin. Some traditional symbols associated with protection include the pentacle, the eye, the ankh, and the cross, depending on your path. You can also create your own sigils for protection by writing out a statement of intent, breaking it down into a design, and charging it with your energy.

Spirit Guides

Some practitioners call on deities, ancestors, or spirit guides for protection. This is usually highly specific to each person and the religion they follow. These allies can be asked to watch over a space, accompany you in difficult moments, or lend strength to your spells. In ancient Jewish Kabbalah, angels are often called upon to banish negative energy and provide protection to the practitioners. In Wicca, many witches call upon elemental forces for guidance and power. Offerings, prayers, or simple words of thanks are just a few ways to help maintain a relationship with these protective forces in your spiritual life.

Mirror Work

Mirrors have long been used in magic for both reflection and reversal. A mirror placed outward in a window is said to deflect negative energy. In personal rituals, a small mirror can be used to reflect harmful intentions back to their source. This is not done with vengeful intent, but as a way of returning any negative energy that is not yours to carry. You can use this principle with mirrors in any of your spellwork or rituals.

Salt and Iron

Both salt and iron have ancient reputations as protective substances. Salt purifies and stabilizes energy, making it ideal for creating sacred space. Iron disrupts harmful spirits and energies. A nail in a doorway or an iron horseshoe above a threshold can serve as a simple but powerful charm.

Protective Crystals

Crystals have long been used in magical traditions for their energetic properties, especially in regards to protection and grounding. You can carry them, place them in your home, wear them as jewelry, or incorporate them into rituals. They are quiet allies that help support your energy field. To activate a crystal for protection, cleanse it first and then charge it with your intention. This can be done by holding it in your hands, speaking your purpose aloud, or visualizing it filled with light. While there are many different types of crystals used for all sorts of purposes, let's briefly cover the crystals most often used for protection and grounding.

Black Tourmaline is one of the most powerful stones for absorbing and transmuting negative energy. It can be placed at entry points to the home, carried in a pocket, or worn for ongoing protection.

Obsidian is volcanic glass known for its ability to form a spiritual shield around anyone who carries it. It is excellent for cutting cords and protecting against psychic attacks.

Hematite offers grounding and stability. It is especially helpful for people who feel scattered or drained by the energies of others.

Smoky Quartz is protective and purifying. It can help transform dense energy into light and is often used in cleansing rituals.

Amethyst, though more commonly associated with clarity and intuition, is also protective, particularly against mental or emotional overwhelm.

PROTECTION MAGIC DOES NOT ALWAYS REQUIRE formal ritual. Many practices can be woven into your daily life. Washing your hands with intention can become a cleansing act. Wearing specific jewelry or colors can act as a shield. Taking a few deep breaths before entering a crowded space can help anchor your energy.

You might begin the day by imagining a golden light surrounding your body like a cloak. You might end the day by brushing off your energy field with your hands and setting the intention to release anything that is not yours. These small acts, done with awareness, can build strong energetic resilience over time.

Protection magic is not about hiding from or escaping your fears. It is about standing in your truth and refusing to be pulled off center no matter what comes your way. It is about saying no when needed, recognizing your worth, and taking responsibility for your energy. In a world full of noise, protection magic helps you remember who you are.

19

THE CHAKRAS

The chakras are an ancient system of energy centers that originate from Indian spiritual traditions. They offer a map of the subtle body and a way to understand the connection between your physical state, emotional well-being, and spiritual awareness. The word "chakra" comes from Sanskrit and means "wheel" or "disk," referring to the spinning energy centers that run along the spine and into the crown of the head. Each chakra is believed to govern specific aspects of your being, from survival and creativity to love, expression, and enlightenment.

While many traditions speak of energy centers in the body, the seven chakra system has become the most well-known in modern spiritual practice. These seven primary chakras are aligned along the central channel of the body, from the base of the spine to the top of the head. Each one is associated with a color, a sound, an element, a set of organs, and a spiritual lesson. When your chakras are open and balanced, energy flows freely and you feel aligned in body, mind, and spirit. When they are blocked or overactive, you may experience physical symptoms, emotional imbalance, or spiritual disconnection.

The Root Chakra

Located at the base of the spine, the root chakra is your foundation. It governs your sense of safety, stability, and belonging in the world. It is associated with the color red and the element of earth. When balanced, the root chakra gives you a sense of grounding, security, and trust in life. You feel supported and connected to your physical body. When blocked, you may feel anxious, disconnected, or constantly afraid. Practices such as walking barefoot on the earth, eating nourishing foods, and focusing on the breath can help bring this chakra into balance. The root chakra reminds you that you are safe, and that you belong here.

The Sacral Chakra

Just below the navel lies the sacral chakra, the center of creativity, sensuality, and emotional flow. Its color is orange, and its element is water. This chakra governs your ability to feel pleasure, express yourself, and form intimate relationships. When in balance, it brings joy, openness, and a healthy connection to desire. When blocked, you may feel emotionally numb, creatively stifled, or out of touch with your body. Movement, dance, time in water, and creative expression are powerful ways to activate this chakra. It teaches you to embrace life's pleasures and to honor your emotions without shame.

The Solar Plexus Chakra

Above the navel sits the solar plexus chakra, your center of willpower, confidence, and personal identity. It is linked with the color yellow and the element of fire. This chakra governs your self-esteem, motivation, and ability to act in the world. When balanced, you feel empowered, decisive, and purposeful. When imbalanced, you may feel powerless, indecisive, or driven by the need for control. Working with the solar plexus involves setting healthy boundaries, taking action, and recognizing your inner strength. It is the fire within you that fuels growth, courage, and transformation.

The Heart Chakra

In the center of the chest is the heart chakra, the bridge between the lower and upper energy centers. It is associated with the color green and the element of air. The heart chakra governs love, compassion, forgiveness, and connection. When balanced, it allows you to give and receive love freely, to empathize with others, and to forgive both yourself and those who have hurt you. When blocked, you may feel closed off, bitter, or fearful of intimacy. Heart-opening meditations, acts of kindness, and deep breathing can help restore balance. This chakra teaches that love is the most powerful force for healing and unity.

The Throat Chakra

Located at the base of the throat, the throat chakra is the center of communication and truth. Its color is blue, and its element is sound. This chakra governs your ability to speak your truth, to listen deeply, and to express your thoughts and feelings clearly. When in balance, it empowers honest expression and aligned action. When blocked, you may feel unheard, silenced, or afraid to speak your mind. Singing, journaling, and mindful conversation are all helpful tools for awakening this chakra. It reminds you that your voice matters, and that truth is sacred.

The Third Eye Chakra

Between the eyebrows lies the third eye chakra, the seat of intuition, insight, and inner vision. It is connected to the color indigo and to the element of light. This chakra governs your ability to see beyond the physical, to perceive patterns, and to access spiritual wisdom. When balanced, it brings clarity, imagination, and deep intuitive knowing.

When blocked, you may feel disconnected from your inner guidance or struggle to trust your instincts. Practices like visualization, dreamwork, and meditation can help open this center. The third eye encourages you to see not just with your eyes, but with your soul.

The Crown Chakra

At the top of the head is the crown chakra, the portal to higher consciousness and divine connection. It is associated with the color violet or pure white, and with the element of ether or spirit. This chakra governs your sense of unity with the universe, your spiritual awareness, and your access to transcendence. When balanced, it brings a deep sense of peace, purpose, and connection to something greater than yourself. When blocked, you may feel spiritually lost, isolated, or overly attached to material concerns. Silent meditation, prayer, and time in nature can help you connect to this center. The crown chakra teaches that you are not separate from the divine, but a part of it.

THE CHAKRA SYSTEM is like a living map that can guide your healing, growth, and spiritual awakening. You do not need to master all seven at once. Often, one chakra will call to you more strongly than the others. Begin where you are. Pay attention to what your body and emotions are telling you. Use the chakras as a way to listen more deeply to yourself.

There is no need to force balance. The chakras respond to your awareness and your intention. Through meditation, breathwork, sound healing, movement, and self-reflection, you can gently bring them into harmony. You can also work with crystals, colors, essential oils, or affirmations that correspond to each center. Whether you follow a structured practice or a more intuitive path, the key is to remain present with yourself.

The chakras remind you that your body is sacred. Your energy is sacred. Every feeling, every instinct, every thought has its place in the landscape of your soul. As you work with this system, you are not just healing individual parts of yourself, but actively awakening the whole. You are remembering that you are already complete, already divine, and already in connection with the energy that moves through all things.

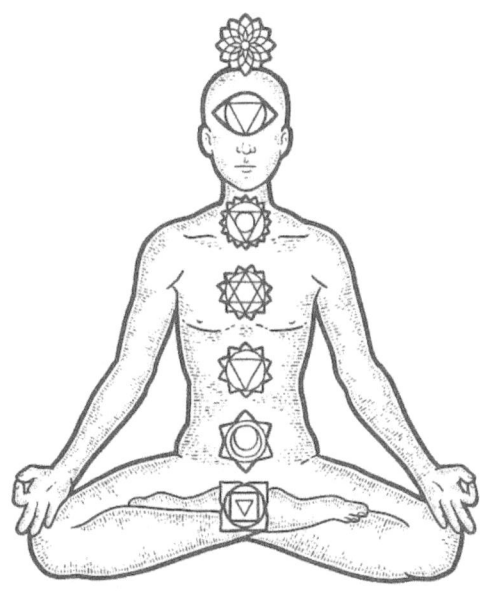

20

HEALING MAGIC

Healing magic is the practice of restoring balance to the body, mind, and spirit through intention, energy, and connection with the natural world. It does not replace medicine, but complements it by addressing the deeper energetic patterns that underlie suffering. Healing magic centers on a belief that the body is both physical and spiritual, with many energetic layers in-between. As a result, true wellness comes from alignment on *all* levels of being.

Throughout history, healing and magic were very closely linked. In ancient temples, sacred groves, and village hearths, healers worked with herbs, touch, ritual, and prayer to ease pain and support recovery. Illness was often seen not only as a biological issue, but also as a sign of disconnection from self, from nature, or from spirit. Healing magic seeks to mend those connections and guide the body back to its natural state of harmony.

Healing begins with attention, presence, and care. Whether you are offering healing to yourself or to another, the first step is to listen. Not to fix or force, but to understand what is out of balance. This might be a physical wound, emotional trauma, energetic blockage, or spiritual numbness. Healing magic asks you to respond gently, patiently, and with respect for the body's own wisdom.

There are many tools used in healing magic. Hands can channel energy. Words can soothe or empower. Water can cleanse. Breath can realign. Fire can release. Touch, scent, sound, and movement all become pathways through which healing flows. Some healing is slow and deep, like roots regrowing. Some is quick and relieving, like a knot untied. Often external tools, like crystals and herbs, are utilized to focus intention and amplify healing energy.

Healing Crystals

Crystals are often used in healing work for their ability to hold and direct subtle energy. Each type of stone has a unique vibration that can support specific needs. Clear quartz is used to amplify healing and restore clarity. Amethyst calms the mind and supports emotional release. Rose quartz encourages love, forgiveness, and emotional healing. Black tourmaline helps release trauma and protect sensitive energy. These stones can be placed on the body, kept nearby during rest, or used in meditation to gently shift energy and support recovery.

Healing Herbs

In magical practice, herbs are chosen not just for their medicinal properties, but for their energetic qualities as well. Chamomile soothes the nervous system and invites peace. Calendula helps the skin heal and brings warmth and comfort. Lavender eases tension and calms the spirit. Peppermint stimulates circulation and clears the mind. These herbs can be used in teas, baths, oils, and poultices, prepared with care and intention. Gathering or preparing herbs while focusing on healing adds power to their effect. Remember that herbal remedies should only be used as a complement to medical treatment, never as a replacement. Always thoroughly research the herbs you use to check for any allergies or conflicts with existing medication you may be taking.

Reiki and Energy Work

Reiki is a form of energy healing that originated in Japan. Practitioners channel universal life force through the hands to support the body's natural healing ability. Reiki is gentle, noninvasive, and deeply relaxing. It can be done in person or at a distance, and often brings emotional release, clarity, or a sense of peace. Some reiki practitioners may even utilize chakra balancing and breathwork during a session. All of these practices involve tuning into the body's energy field, sensing where it is blocked or depleted, and using focused intention to restore flow.

HEALING MAGIC DOES NOT HAVE to be complicated. It can be as simple as placing your hand over your heart, taking a deep breath, and whispering words of love to yourself. It can be lighting a candle for someone in pain, making a meal with herbs that nurture the body, or walking barefoot on the earth to ground and recharge. What makes it magical is the intention, the presence, and the belief that healing is possible.

Some healing cannot be rushed. There are wounds that ask to be witnessed rather than fixed. In these cases, healing magic is about holding space, offering comfort, and allowing the slow process of transformation to unfold. Healing may not always mean curing. Sometimes it means softening, integrating, or learning how to carry pain differently. It may mean finding beauty in your scars or reclaiming a sense of wholeness even while you are still in process.

To practice healing magic is to become a vessel of compassion. You will learn to recognize the sacredness of the body, the intelligence of nature, and the quiet power of love and care. You will start to put faith in the body's marvelous capacity to mend. Healing does not have to be dramatic. Often it looks like resting when needed, speaking kindly to yourself, or choosing food that nourishes your energy. These small acts, repeated with intention, become rituals of care. They remind us that every wound also holds the possibility of a return to wholeness.

SECTION III:
ADVANCED MAGIC

"The most beautiful thing we can experience is the mysterious.
It is the source of all true art and all science."

— Albert Einstein

ALCHEMY

Alchemy is a branch of magical and philosophical thought concerned with self transformation. Often misunderstood as a primitive form of chemistry, alchemy is much more than the pursuit of gold from lead. For practitioners of advanced magic, alchemy is the art of transforming matter, spirit, and self. It is both a spiritual path and a scientific discipline meant to bring about real, measurable change.

Although alchemy rose to prominence in medieval Europe, its origins reach back much further. Ancient Egypt practiced a proto-alchemical art called *khemeia*, concerned with death, rebirth, and divine transformation. In China, Taoist alchemists developed inner alchemy (*neidan*) focused on longevity and the cultivation of spiritual essence. India contributed through Ayurvedic and Tantric traditions, linking material transmutation with energy centers in the body. Though the symbols, terminology, and methods for alchemy varied across cultures, they all shared a common belief that the material and spiritual worlds are deeply intertwined.

Western alchemy really began to flourish during the Middle Ages and Renaissance, when classical philosophy was fused with Hermeticism, Gnosticism, and Christian mysticism. During this time, alchemists would lock themselves away in secret laboratories, performing experiments and writing manuals rich with cryptic illustrations and symbolic language. Their texts were filled with images of dragons, lions, suns, and moons, each thought to be codes for universal forces. These were not just science experiments, but rituals of transformation meant to align the practitioner with divine will.

To the alchemist, every physical operation reflected an inner process. The transformation of lead into gold was symbolic of a greater goal: the refinement of the soul. Through fire, dissolution, and recombination, the practitioner sought to purify the self and awaken spiritual wisdom. This ultimate goal of alchemical transformation came to be known as the Great Work.

The Great Work

The Great Work is the central aim of alchemy. It is the journey of turning base material into gold, not just in the crucible but in the soul. It represents the refinement of the self through trials, insight, and devotion. The Great Work teaches that within every person lies both the lead of ignorance and the gold of enlightenment. Through conscious effort and spiritual practice, the lower can be transformed into the higher.

Alchemists divided the Great Work into several stages, each symbolizing a step in the process of inner and outer transformation. Though the exact order varies between traditions, four primary stages are often described.

Nigredo, or blackening, represents the breaking down of the old self. It is a time of dissolution, confusion, and decay. This is the shadow stage, where false identities are burned away and illusions are stripped. In life, this often corresponds to a period of crisis, grief, or loss that forces deep self-reflection.

Albedo, or whitening, is the stage of purification. After the darkness of nigredo, the seeker begins to recover clarity and peace. Old wounds are cleansed. The self becomes more conscious and balanced. This is a time of healing and realignment.

Citrinitas, or yellowing, symbolizes awakening. Insight dawns. The inner fire is rekindled. The soul begins to shine with a sense of purpose and understanding. It is often seen as the dawning of wisdom and spiritual maturity.

Rubedo, or reddening, is the final stage of integration. The opposites within the self are united. Spirit and matter become one. This is the completion of The Great Work, where the self has been completely reborn. It is the stage of inner gold, known by some as the philosopher's stone.

These stages are not always linear. A person may cycle through them many times in a lifetime. The Great Work is not a goal to be reached once, but an unfolding process of becoming. It is a lifelong internal battle for order over chaos.

The Legacy of Alchemy

Alchemy is still practiced today, and remains one of the most fascinating blends of science and mysticism in human history. Alchemists saw nature as a mirror of the soul and believed that the study of transformation in the physical world could teach us secrets of the spirit. Many described their laboratories as sacred spaces where divine truths revealed themselves through the behavior of metals and fire.

The influence of alchemy can be seen across many spiritual and magical traditions. It shaped the development of ceremonial magic, influenced early science, and laid the foundation for depth psychology. Carl Jung, one of the most influential psychologists of the twentieth century, drew heavily from alchemical imagery in his theories of individuation and shadow work. He saw alchemy as a symbolic map of the psyche and believed that its processes mirrored the path toward wholeness.

Modern practitioners of alchemy continue to use these symbols as tools for meditation, ritual, and self-exploration. The language of alchemy offers a powerful way to understand personal growth, trauma, healing, and enlightenment. It teaches that suffering is not wasted, but rather an integral part of the fire that refines the soul. It reminds us that we are not fixed beings, but ever-changing forms of potential.

Alchemy can be practiced through journaling, dreamwork, meditation, visualization, and symbolic ritual. A person may choose to explore each stage of the Great Work in their own life, identifying where they are and what is being asked of them. A dark period may be seen not as failure, but as the nigredo, or a necessary breaking down before rebirth. A time of clarity may be the albedo, or a signal that healing has begun. Through this lens, life itself becomes an alchemical process.

Alchemy teaches that you are both the crucible and the flame. You are the lead and the gold. You are the work, the worker, and the reward. It is to see every struggle as a step in the refinement of your soul. It is to believe that there is gold in you, waiting to be revealed through patience and presence. Through this sacred act of magic, you will unlock endless possibilities for personal growth and a real path towards spiritual enlightenment.

CEREMONIAL MAGIC

C eremonial magic is without a doubt the most structured and symbolically rich branch of the magical arts. It involves precise rituals, sacred tools, and complex systems designed to align the practitioner with spiritual forces. Unlike intuitive forms of spellwork, ceremonial magic emphasizes preparation, hierarchy, and tradition. Every gesture, word, and symbol must have intentional meaning and purpose. The goal is not just to influence the material world, but also to bring the soul into harmony with its highest spiritual potential.

The roots of ceremonial magic can be traced to many ancient cultures, including Egypt, Babylon, Greece, and early Jewish mysticism. Modern practice, however, uses a blend of classical philosophy, Christian mysticism, and Renaissance esotericism. The grimoire tradition of medieval Europe played a significant role in shaping this modern interpretation, offering detailed instructions on invoking angels, spirits, and planetary forces. Later, during the nineteenth and twentieth centuries, ceremonial magic was refined into the systems we now associate with groups like the Hermetic Order of the Golden Dawn, the Thelemic movement, and various Kabbalistic schools. These groups provide a rigid hierarchy of structured progression through which a practitioner may gain access to esoteric knowledge or complete increasingly complex rituals to align with their higher self.

Ceremonial magic is often referred to as "high magic." This term does not imply superiority over other traditions, but instead reflects its focus on spiritual elevation and inner transformation. Rituals are designed as symbolic journeys, allowing the practitioner to move closer to divine truth and personal mastery. This work may include invoking spiritual beings, banishing unwanted energies, constructing sacred space, and aligning with planetary or elemental forces. Tools such as the wand, chalice, robe, and altar are essential components of ceremonial magic. Each represents an archetypal force or inner faculty that the magician seeks to awaken and embody.

The complexity of ceremonial magic may seem daunting to beginners, but it offers a deep and transformative path for those drawn to structure and symbolism. While some aspects are rooted in historical tradition, others have evolved to meet the needs of modern practitioners. Today, ceremonial magic is practiced by solitary magicians, small study groups, and organized orders around the world, all with a common goal of awakening the human soul to its ultimate potential.

The Kabbalah

One of the central influences on ceremonial magic is the Kabbalah, a system of Jewish mysticism that seeks to understand the nature of God, the structure of the universe, and the spiritual destiny of the human soul. Traditional Kabbalistic teachings are rooted in sacred Jewish texts, such as the *Zohar* and the *Sefer Yetzirah*, which explore creation as a process of divine emanation and spiritual unfolding.

At the heart of the Kabbalah is the Tree of Life, a symbolic diagram composed of ten spheres called sephirot, each representing a divine attribute or stage of manifestation. These include concepts like mercy, strength, beauty, wisdom, and understanding. The sephirot are connected by twenty-two paths, which correspond to the letters of

the Hebrew alphabet and, in later Western adaptations, to the major
arcana of the tarot. The Tree is meant to function as both a map of
the cosmos and a mirror of the human soul, charting the descent of
divinity into the material world and offering a pathway for the seeker's return to spiritual wholeness.

Kabbalah teaches that by contemplating the sephirot, meditating
on divine names, and exploring the relationships between symbols,
numbers, and sounds, a practitioner can come into deeper alignment
with the divine will and gain insight into their higher purpose. In
ceremonial magic, the Tree of Life becomes the central framework
for organizing rituals, spiritual correspondences, and inner work.
Each sephira is associated with specific angels, planetary energies,
magical tools, and symbolic colors, allowing the magician to
construct detailed rituals that move energy intentionally through the
spiritual hierarchy.

While traditional Kabbalah is a theological and initiatory system
within Judaism, its ideas were adapted by Western occultists during
the Renaissance and later formalized into what is now known as
Hermetic Kabbalah. This version blends Kabbalistic symbolism with
Christian mysticism, Neoplatonic philosophy, astrology, and alchemical imagery. Though it differs significantly from its Jewish origins,
Hermetic Kabbalah has become a foundational system within
Western esotericism, especially in ceremonial magic. It serves as a
universal symbolic language through which spiritual forces are
understood, invoked, and embodied.

Rosicrucianism

Rosicrucianism is a mystical and philosophical tradition that
emerged in Europe in the early seventeenth century. It presents itself
as the legacy of a secret brotherhood devoted to spiritual enlightenment, the study of nature, and the inner transformation of the self.
While the true origins of the Rosicrucians remain mysterious, the
movement was introduced to the public through a series of anony-
mous manifestos: the *Fama Fraternitatis* (1614), the *Confessio Fraterni-*

tatis (1615), and the *Chymical Wedding of Christian Rosenkreuz* (1616). These texts described the life and teachings of a mythical figure named Christian Rosenkreuz, who symbolized the ideal of an enlightened practitioner.

Rosicrucian philosophy blends Christian mysticism, Hermeticism, alchemy, astrology, and elements of Kabbalah. It emphasizes personal revelation, the perfection of the soul, and the harmony between science, nature, and spirit. Unlike mainstream religious doctrine, Rosicrucianism advocates a direct and experiential relationship with divine truth, guided by symbolic wisdom and inner initiation.

The Rosicrucian worldview is also deeply allegorical. Symbols such as the rose (representing divine love and spiritual unfolding) and the cross (representing earthly trials and transformation) are central to its teachings. The spiritual path of the Rosicrucian is one of disciplined study, ethical living, and inner purification, ultimately with the goal of direct union with divine forces.

Though the original brotherhood may never have existed in a literal sense, Rosicrucianism profoundly shaped the development of Western esotericism. It inspired later magical and philosophical systems, including Freemasonry, alchemy, and ceremonial magic. Many of the symbolic structures and cosmological ideas found in Rosicrucian texts later appeared in the teachings of the Hermetic Order of the Golden Dawn and similar groups.

Modern Rosicrucian organizations, such as AMORC (the Ancient Mystical Order Rosae Crucis), continue to preserve and adapt these teachings for contemporary seekers. While each group interprets the tradition differently, the essence remains the same: a commitment to spiritual awakening, the pursuit of hidden knowledge, and the cultivation of wisdom through symbol, meditation, and service.

Freemasonry

Freemasonry is a fraternal and philosophical order that rose to prominence in the seventeenth and eighteenth centuries, though its symbolic and mythological roots stretch back much further. While its public face is that of a moral and charitable society, Freemasonry is also an initiatory tradition that preserves layers of esoteric symbolism, allegory, and ritual. Its influence on Western ceremonial magic has been far-reaching, shaping the development of numerous magical systems and traditions that followed.

The teachings of Freemasonry are conveyed through a series of degrees, each representing a stage of moral, intellectual, and spiritual refinement. These degrees are enacted through elaborate initiation rituals rich with symbolic gestures, sacred geometry, architectural metaphors, and references to ancient mystery traditions. The central myth of Masonic lore often revolves around the building of Solomon's Temple, which serves as a metaphor for constructing the inner temple of the self.

Freemasonry emphasizes personal integrity, inner discipline, and the pursuit of truth. Its symbols, such as the compass and square, the all-seeing eye, and the rough and smooth ashlars, represent tools for self-mastery and spiritual development. Though not overtly magical, the Masonic system operates through ritual drama, intending to initiate transformation in the consciousness of the practitioner through symbolic experience.

There are many branches of Freemasonry, including the Blue Lodge, which confers the first three degrees, and higher or side orders such as the Scottish Rite and York Rite, which introduce additional layers of mysticism, biblical allegory, and philosophical insight. Some of these rites contain elements derived from Rosicrucianism, alchemy, and Kabbalah, pointing to an underlying esoteric current within the broader Masonic framework.

Many early occultists and ceremonial magicians were also Freemasons, and they adapted Masonic structures and ideals into their magical systems. The Hermetic Order of the Golden Dawn, for example, borrowed heavily from Masonic degree systems, officer roles, and ritual forms while incorporating a wider range of mystical and magical elements. Thus, Freemasonry stands as a pivotal link between mystical philosophy and modern ceremonial magic.

The Hermetic Order of the Golden Dawn

The Hermetic Order of the Golden Dawn was one of the most influential magical societies of the modern era. Founded in the late nineteenth century in Britain by a group of Freemasons and occult scholars, the Golden Dawn synthesized various esoteric traditions into a single, highly structured system of ceremonial magic. Drawing from Kabbalah, astrology, tarot, alchemy, geomancy, Rosicrucianism, and ancient Egyptian symbolism, the order provided a comprehensive framework for magical study and spiritual transformation.

Initiation in the Golden Dawn was organized into a series of graded degrees, each representing a different level of understanding and spiritual progress. These initiations served as ritual enactments of the soul's journey through the Tree of Life. As initiates advanced through the grades, they studied and performed increasingly complex rituals, each designed to refine the self and awaken latent spiritual faculties.

Golden Dawn rituals are highly structured and symbolic. The Lesser Banishing Ritual of the Pentagram (LBRP) is one of its foundational practices, used to purify space and establish energetic boundaries before any magical work. Other rites involve invoking planetary forces, channeling the energies of elemental beings, or traveling on the astral plane through the sephirot of the Tree of Life. Ritual implements such as robes, wands, pentacles, and elemental weapons were carefully designed and consecrated to resonate with specific magical forces.

The Golden Dawn trained and inspired many key figures in modern Western occultism, including Aleister Crowley, Arthur Edward Waite, and Dion Fortune, all of whom went on to shape new traditions and interpretations of ceremonial magic. Although the original order eventually fragmented, its legacy continues through successor organizations, personal practitioners, and an extensive body of written teachings. For many, the Golden Dawn remains a cornerstone of ceremonial magic, offering a disciplined approach to personal transformation and mystical insight.

Thelema

Thelema is a modern spiritual philosophy and magical system developed by Aleister Crowley in the early twentieth century. It centers on the principle: "*Do what thou wilt shall be the whole of the Law. Love is the law, love under will.*" At the heart of Thelema is the idea that every individual has a True Will, which is a unique spiritual purpose or path that reflects their deepest nature and highest destiny. The work of magicians in Thelema is ultimately to discover, embrace, and fully express this Will.

Thelema blends ceremonial magic with mysticism, yoga, meditation, astrology, and Eastern philosophy. It draws on elements of the Golden Dawn system while adding its own rituals, symbols, and cosmology. The core text of Thelema is *The Book of the Law*, which Crowley claimed to have received through direct spiritual transmission in 1904. Additional foundational texts include *Liber Samekh*, a ritual for achieving contact with the Holy Guardian Angel, and *Liber Resh*, a solar adoration practice performed four times daily to align with cosmic cycles.

In Thelemic practice, the magician is not merely a servant of spiritual powers, but an expression of divine creative force. Rituals often involve the invocation of deities, angels, or spiritual archetypes to aid in self-realization and inner awakening. Practices such as the assumption of god-forms, pathworking, and symbolic initiations are used to transform consciousness and align the practitioner with higher planes of existence.

Thelema emphasizes personal responsibility, discipline, and direct experience over rigid dogma. Its rituals are designed to awaken the divine spark within, revealing the magician as both student and embodiment of spiritual law. Though Crowley remains a highly controversial figure, his influence on modern occultism is still felt to this day.

Ceremonial Witchcraft

While ceremonial magic is often associated with structured orders and arcane systems, it also exists within modern witchcraft traditions. Ceremonial witchcraft combines the personal, intuitive elements of folk magic with the disciplined ritual structure found in high magic. It brings together the sacredness of space, the symbolism of tools, and the power of intention into a form of ritual that is both spiritual and transformative.

At the center of ceremonial witchcraft is the ritual circle. Casting a circle creates a boundary between the everyday world and the realm of spirit. It is a space that is both protected and empowered, where magical forces can be safely summoned, worked with, and released. The circle is often imagined as a sphere of light or energy that surrounds the practitioner, acting as a form of protection magic. Many who cast a circle around themselves report feeling a tangible shift in the atmosphere, whether that be an increase in stillness, focus, or presence.

To cast a ritual circle, the practitioner begins by cleansing the space. This may involve sweeping the area with a broom, burning herbs like sage or rosemary, or ringing a bell to clear stagnant energy. Once the space is prepared, the magician walks the perimeter with a tool such as a wand, athame, or staff, drawing the boundary with intention. As they move clockwise, they may invoke the elements at the four cardinal directions: earth in the north, air in the east, fire in the south, and water in the west. Some also call upon the spirit or center, completing the fivefold structure of the pentacle.

Each direction represents a different quality or power. Earth brings stability and grounding. Air brings clarity and communication. Fire brings passion and transformation. Water brings intuition and healing. Spirit unites them all and acts as the divine presence within the ritual. These forces are treated as living energies that the witch enters into a relationship with. As you can see, this form of ceremonial magic overlaps greatly with both elemental magic and protective warding.

Inside the circle, an altar is constructed to act as the heart of the ritual. It may hold candles, representations of the elements, magical tools, herbs, and objects connected to the purpose of the working. Every item has meaning. Every action is intentional. Whether the goal is healing, protection, divination, or celebration, the ritual is crafted with care. Words are often spoken aloud to direct energy, call on spiritual allies, or affirm desires. Movement, visualization, and breathwork are also common tools within ceremonial witchcraft.

One of the most well-known rituals that uses a circle is the full moon rite. Witches gather under the moon to honor its power, reflect on their path, and raise energy for personal or collective goals. The circle becomes a container for that energy, which is raised through chanting, dancing, drumming, or meditation and then directed toward a specific intention. Once the ritual is complete, the energy is grounded, often by touching the earth or sharing food, and the circle is opened by walking counterclockwise and thanking each elemental force.

Ceremonial witchcraft is both serious and creative. It draws from older traditions but encourages personal adaptation. A ritual may follow a set structure but still be tailored to your own practice. What matters is not perfection, but focus and presence. The circle becomes a mirror for the self, a temple for spirit, and a gateway between worlds. It is a place where the sacred becomes tangible and the unseen becomes felt. In this way, ceremonial witchcraft brings together the best of both worlds. It honors tradition without being arbitrarily bound by it. Some may find that the lack of rigid structure in ceremonial witchcraft is actually a deterrent, and that is completely fine too! What matters most is finding a system that works best with your personal and spiritual goals.

RITUAL DESIGN

R itual is the container through which magic becomes action. In ceremonial magic, you've seen how structured, symbolic acts can focus energy and create powerful transformation, but you don't need to follow a formal system to access this power.

Designing your own ritual is an act of sacred authorship. It allows you to weave intention, symbolism, and energy into a personalized form that reflects your unique spiritual language. This chapter offers a framework for crafting personalized rituals so you can start practicing magic in your daily life.

If you feel drawn to a specific religious framework, your rituals can be designed within that structure. Some people may see this as a departure from tradition, but I see it as a sign that you are beginning to trust your own intuition and spiritual voice.

Begin with Clear Intention

Every spell or ritual begins with intention. This is the energetic seed from which everything grows. Ask yourself: *"What am I trying to shift, heal, call in, or release?"* The clearer your intention, the more focused your energy will be. Try to state your intention in the simplest, most direct terms possible. For example:

I release fear and open to trust.
I call in abundance and financial stability.
I ask for healing in my body and mind.
I honor the end of a chapter and welcome what's next.

Intention should be a clear and formal declaration. Write it down or say it aloud. Feel it in your body and believe it in your soul.

Choose Correspondences Thoughtfully

Once your intention is clear, begin selecting elements that resonate with it. These are often called correspondences: tools, colors, herbs, symbols, or planetary energies that align with your goal. Below are some common correspondences.

Protection: black candles, obsidian, rosemary, iron nails, salt, Mars.

Love: rose petals, pink or red cloth, honey, copper, rose quartz, Venus.

Clarity: white candles, clear quartz, mint, the moon, air, lavender.

Abundance: green cloth, basil, coins, cinnamon, pyrite, Jupiter.

Healing: blue candles, chamomile, amethyst, water, aloe, sunflowers.

Confidence: gold, sunstone, cinnamon, tiger's eye, orange candles.

Banishing: black salt, onyx, wormwood, bells, waning moon, Saturn.

Creativity: orange candles, marigold, citrine, Mercury.

Intuition: purple candles, frankincense, amethyst, feathers, Neptune.

You don't need every possible correspondence, just choose a few that hold meaning for you. If money is an issue, you can simply imagine these items in your mind's eye. The key is not perfection, but resonance. Use what's accessible, and remember that your belief and focus are what empower the tools.

Structure Your Ritual

While there are no hard rules, most rituals follow a basic rhythm. As you gain experience, you'll begin to notice common patterns across them. A ritual usually consists of the following steps, in the order they appear:

Preparation – Cleanse your space and gather materials. Some people take a ritual bath, ground their energy, or light incense to shift into sacred space.

Opening – Call in your spiritual allies, deities, elements, or simply acknowledge the sacredness of the space.

Statement of Intent – Speak your intention clearly and confidently. This can be a simple phrase, a chant, or even a poetic invocation.

Symbolic Intent – This is the active part of a ritual: lighting a candle, writing a sigil, burying an object, anointing your body. Choose a symbolic action that gives form to your goal. It can be a single action or a complex set of steps.

Raising Energy – Channel your focus and emotion into the work. You might chant, dance, drum, sing, breathe deeply, or visualize your goal manifesting. Energy is what powers your intention.

Release and Grounding – Let go of the magic and trust the universe to carry it forward. You might blow out a candle, bury an object, pour out water, or offer thanks.

Closing – Thank the spirits, elements, or energies you invoked. Close the space with gratitude and return to ordinary consciousness.

This structure can be as simple or as elaborate as you like. What matters is that each step feels intentional and clear. It may help to physically write the steps down on paper as you brainstorm.

Keep a Record

Start a spellbook or grimoire to document your ideas and rituals. Write down your process, your intention, what you used, and what happened after. This will not only help you refine your practice, but also give you a tangible record of your growth as a practitioner. Over time, this book becomes a magical artifact in its own right.

Trust Your Inner Voice

The most important lesson in developing your own practice is this: trust yourself. You are not required to follow someone else's script. If a chant doesn't feel right, rewrite it. If a traditional tool doesn't resonate, substitute it. You are the co-creator of your spiritual path. Let your intuition be your guide. Most of all, don't be afraid to make mistakes or change your mind.

24

DREAMWORK

Throughout human history, dreams have served as a bridge between the conscious and the unconscious, acting as one of the few visual insights to the inner self. Experienced across every culture and tradition, dreams have long been revered as portals to deeper realms of knowledge, self-reflection, and metaphysical experience. Modern science has not yet been able to figure out a compelling reason for *why* we dream, but mystics have long since understood them as messages. For the spiritual awakened, dreams can serve as powerful insight from the divine.

To cultivate an intentional relationship with dreams is to participate in the ancient spiritual practice of dreamwork. Such work can expand awareness, deepen intuition, and foster a sense of personal revelation. Whether through interpretation or lucid dreaming, the dream world offers a vast and personal terrain for exploration of your inner self.

Interpreting Dreams

The process of dream interpretation attempts to engage with the symbolic language of the unconscious mind. While much of our society treats dreams as either meaningless or superficial, many spiritual and psychological traditions view them as encoded expressions of deep internal processes, unresolved emotions, and archetypal forces.

The first step in working with dreams is recollection. You can start by creating consistent rituals around sleep and awakening. Keeping a dream journal beside your bed and recording details immediately upon waking strengthens your ability to remember, and later analyze, the content of your dream. Even fragmented impressions (an image, word, or sensation) can hold significance. Over time, recurrent symbols and motifs may emerge, offering clues to the dreamer's inner life.

While archetypal symbols can be helpful reference points, effective interpretation demands a deeply personal approach. The meaning of a river, a snake, or a locked door will vary depending on the dreamer's experiences, cultural background, and emotional associations. Attention should be paid not only to the literal elements, but to the affective tone of the dream and the intuitive emotions it evokes.

Dreams often engage unresolved conflicts, latent fears, or spiritual callings. In certain cases, they may function as visions, messages from ancestors, guides, or aspects of the self that are not easily accessible during waking consciousness. The dream realm thus becomes a sacred text, written in the language of metaphor, and requiring the same patience, reverence, and discernment that one might bring to the study of scripture or myth.

Dreamcatchers

Originating from the spiritual traditions of the Ojibwe people and adopted by other Native American communities, dreamcatchers are ritual objects constructed to influence the quality of dreams. They are traditionally composed of a wooden hoop made of willow, interwoven with a web of sinew, and adorned with feathers and beads. The symbolic intention is set to act as a filter between the dreamer and the spiritual influences of the night.

In their original cultural context, dreamcatchers are not decorations, but sacred tools. It is believed that beneficial dreams pass through the central opening, descending gently along the feathers to the sleeper below, while disruptive or malevolent dreams are trapped in the web and disintegrated by the morning light. Each component of the dreamcatcher carries meaning. The circular frame represents the cyclical nature of life and the cosmos, while the web echoes the delicate intricacy of spiritual communication.

In modern spiritual practice, dreamcatchers may be employed as part of a broader ritual of psychic protection or dream incubation. When treated with intention, they can function as energetic wards and anchors for deeper dreamwork. However, it is essential to approach their use with cultural sensitivity and an acknowledgment of their indigenous origins. We must recognize that appropriating sacred objects without the proper understanding or respect significantly undermines their power. If you do attempt to purchase a dreamcatcher, try to only support Native American owned businesses. Always avoid factories that mass-produce appropriated items for profit.

Lucid Dreaming

Lucid dreaming is the phenomenon wherein an individual becomes consciously aware within the dream state. In this heightened condition of self-awareness, the dreamer may exert influence over the dream environment, engage in dialogue with dream figures, or pursue specific actions with volition. It is a state where the veil between waking agency and dream consciousness becomes permeable.

The capacity for lucidity can be cultivated through a variety of techniques. Among the most effective are dream journaling, reality testing throughout the day, and setting firm intentions before sleep. Common induction methods include visualization exercises, mnemonic triggers, and setting alarms to disrupt the sleep cycle and reintroduce conscious awareness during entry into the rapid eye movement phase of sleep. For some, lucid dreams may occur randomly without even trying. Some people lucid dream all the time without any effort, while others may never experience one in their life.

If you do eventually find yourself in a lucid dream, you can use the opportunity to confront your fears, rehearse real-world scenarios, engage in symbolic ritual, or explore creative and mystical experiences that transcend the limits of the waking mind. Unlike traditional dreams, lucid dreams offer a participatory role in the construction and navigation of the dreamscape. Since it is *your* mind, you have complete control over the experience.

Some people choose to directly incorporate lucid dreaming into their spiritual practice. Rather than treating it as a novelty or psychological trick, they see it as a form of sacred ritual. Within the dream state, one may find themselves in direct contact with inner guides, ancestors, or spiritual beings. These encounters can offer clarity, healing, or teachings that feel just as meaningful, if not more so, than those received in waking life. In this way, lucid dreaming has the potential to allow for unlimited exploration of the unconscious mind.

25

ASTRAL PROJECTION

Astral projection is the intentional shifting of consciousness beyond the confines of the physical body. Sometimes called an "out-of-body experience", it is a technique through which practitioners claim to separate from the material form and travel through spiritual realms. This journey does not involve physical movement, but rather a deep inward shift during meditation to open access to the astral plane of existence. It is one of the most enigmatic practices found in the spiritual arts.

Astral projection is mostly about expanding your conscious awareness. In many esoteric traditions, it is believed that each person possesses multiple energetic bodies layered over the physical. The astral body, or subtle double, is thought to be the vessel of consciousness during these journeys. In projection, this body detaches from the physical and moves freely through what is often called the astral plane—a dimension shaped by thought, energy, and spirit.

Most accounts of astral travel begin with a state of deep stillness. The body is completely relaxed, sometimes on the edge of sleep, while the mind remains lucid. This threshold is known as the hypnagogic state, and it is in this liminal space that the shift begins. Practitioners may report intense vibrations, auditory anomalies such as ringing or buzzing, or the sense of being lifted, pulled, or unmoored. The moment of separation can feel sudden or gradual, and it often carries a sensation of disorientation before clarity arrives.

Techniques for inducing astral projection vary across traditions. Some rely on visualizing the self climbing a rope, rolling out of the body, or floating upward. Others use rhythmic breathing, guided meditation, or sound frequencies to induce the right brainwave state. Consistency, patience, and mental discipline are essential if you ever hope to see results. This is not a casual activity, but a skill that must be trained like a muscle. The more you cultivate stillness and focus, the easier it becomes to cross the threshold with your mind.

The experiences people report during astral projection are wildly diverse. Some describe watching their physical body from above, floating in the room, or drifting out into familiar environments. Others find themselves in entirely different landscapes, described as vivid worlds with colors, sounds, and symbols that defy ordinary explanation. Encounters with spiritual beings, ancestral guides, or elemental forces are not uncommon. In many cases, the traveler receives insight, healing, or clarity not easily accessible in waking life. These journeys can feel hyperreal and full of significance, like a psychedelic trip.

From a metaphysical perspective, astral projection suggests that consciousness is not rooted in the brain alone. It points to the possibility that the self is multidimensional, capable of navigating realms that exist beyond space and time. Whether understood as a literal journey or a symbolic vision, the experience opens up a deeper exploration of what it means to be alive, aware, and connected to something greater.

Because of the openness and sensitivity required for this kind of work, preparation is critical. Practitioners often begin with grounding practices to stabilize their energy and clear emotional clutter. Protective rituals, such as invoking sacred symbols, surrounding oneself with light, or calling on spiritual allies can help establish safe boundaries before departure. Maintaining a calm and balanced inner state makes it easier to navigate whatever arises. Upon return, grounding once again is essential. This might include eating grounding foods, engaging in movement, or connecting with the earth through breath and touch.

Skeptics often interpret astral projection as a form of lucid dreaming or a neurological quirk. Indeed, the boundary between the two is quite thin, but for those with experience, astral projection is often described as distinctly separate from dreams; more deliberate, more vivid, and often imbued with spiritual meaning. Whether you believe it reflects an external reality or an inner truth, its impact can still have a profound effect on your life.

To engage in astral travel is to participate in an ancient lineage of seekers, mystics, and visionaries. In cultures around the world, from the shamans of the Amazon to the yogis of India, the practice of soul flight has long been used to retrieve knowledge, perform healing, and connect with the divine. For these people, it is the sacred method of piercing the veil between worlds.

Approach this practice with humility. Be curious, but cautious. Not every realm is welcoming, and not every message is meant for you. Keep a journal of your experiences. Learn your symbols. Know your boundaries. Astral projection is not about abandoning the physical world, but learning how to better inhabit your full being (physical, energetic, and spiritual). As you practice, your soul will remember how to wander. That wandering will help you discover inner truths unreachable by any other path.

26

SEX MAGIC

Sex magic is the practice of using sexual energy as a force for spiritual transformation, manifestation, and magical intention. It is based on the belief that sexual energy is one of the most potent forms of life force available to human beings. When directed with purpose, it can be used to raise energy, unlock higher states of consciousness, and channel powerful desires into reality.

Across history, sacred sexuality has played a role in spiritual traditions from many different cultures. In ancient Mesopotamia and Canaan, temple priestesses used erotic ritual as a form of communion with the divine. In the Indian tantric tradition, sexuality was seen as a sacred path to union with the self, the universe, and the divine. Egyptian and Greek mystery schools also taught forms of erotic mysticism, where the body was not seen as sinful but as a vessel of sacred power.

In modern magical systems, sex magic has been explored by figures like Aleister Crowley and other occultists of the early twentieth century. They developed structured rituals where sexual energy was consciously built, directed, and released in alignment with magical goals. But sex magic is not limited to ceremonial practice. It can be as simple and personal as a moment of focused intention at the height of arousal, or a deep act of loving presence with oneself or a partner.

Sex magic requires a deep emotional intelligence and an appreciation for symbolism. It *can* be about physical pleasure, but most important is the intention behind the experience. Pleasure can become a sacred tool rather than a distraction if used properly. The body becomes an altar, and orgasm becomes a moment of transcendence. Through this peak of energy, the mind and spirit are opened, and intention can be planted like a seed in fertile ground.

Sex magic can be practiced alone or with a partner. Solo practice allows for deep introspection, control, and personal empowerment. Partnered sex magic requires trust, consent, and shared purpose. It is important to approach these practices with clear boundaries, honesty, and emotional maturity. Manipulation, coercion, or spiritual bypassing have no place in sacred sexual work.

One of the simplest forms of solo sex magic involves setting a clear intention before beginning. This may be a goal, a wish, or a spiritual question. As arousal builds, the practitioner focuses completely on this intention. At the moment of orgasm, the energy is released into the universe along with the focused thought. Some may visualize the intention entering a candle flame, a bowl of water, or simply see it moving outward into the world.

Partnered sex magic follows a similar structure, but requires alignment between those involved. Both partners may set the same intention, focus together on the energy being raised, and release it at the moment of climax. Some practitioners use breathwork, eye gazing, chanting, or physical symbols to strengthen the ritual. Afterward, rest and integration are essential. The energy raised can continue to unfold for days or weeks.

Sex magic is not only for manifesting external desires; It is also a powerful tool for healing and transformation. Traumas stored in the body can be gently released through intentional erotic work. Feelings of shame, disconnection, or powerlessness can be dissolved when sexual energy is reclaimed and honored as sacred.

It is important to acknowledge that sex magic, like any spiritual practice, must be rooted in consent and care. It is not a way to bind others, override their will, or force outcomes. The energy raised through sex magic is most effective when it arises from love, clarity, and deep presence. Respect for yourself, your partners, and the forces you work with is essential.

Some practitioners work with primal or archetypal energies in sex magic. These may include divine masculine and feminine aspects, gods and goddesses of love and desire, or even animal totems to represent ancient power. Aphrodite, Eros, Lilith, Pan, and Freya are among the many beings who have been honored in erotic rites. Inviting such energies into your practice can make your rituals feel deeply personal and emotionally vulnerable.

Ritual tools for sex magic may include scented oils, red or pink candles, rose quartz, mirrors, music, or sacred garments. These are not required, but they can help to shift the mind into a focused state. Creating a dedicated space for this work, whether a bedroom altar or a drawn bath, signals to your spirit that something sacred is about to take place. In a world where sexuality is often shamed or exploited, reclaiming it as a sacred force is a radical act. Sex magic can help us to honor our bodies, know our desires, and better appreciate the sacred act of conception.

CHAOS MAGIC

C haos magic is a modern system of magical practice that emphasizes belief as a tool rather than a fixed truth. It teaches that reality can be shaped by the mind, and that the most effective magic is whatever works for the practitioner. Unlike traditional systems with rigid rules or ancient lineages, chaos magic encourages experimentation, flexibility, and personal authority. It is a path for those who are willing to question everything, including their own beliefs.

The roots of chaos magic can be traced back to the late twentieth century, particularly the writings of British occultists like Peter J Carroll and Ray Sherwin. Their work emerged out of dissatisfaction with the limitations of ceremonial magic and traditional occult systems. Drawing from psychology, art, science, and mysticism, they proposed a radically open-ended approach to magic that placed emphasis on results rather than dogma.

A key component of chaos magic is the use of "belief" a spiritual tool. In this context, beliefs are no longer a part of your identity. They are seen as temporary lenses through which we interact with the world. In this way, a chaos magician can adopt a belief for a ritual and discard it afterward. One day they might work with a deity from

Norse mythology, while the next they might design a ritual around a fictional character or a mathematical symbol. Chaos magicians argue that what matters most is the emotional and mental focus that a belief generates, not whether the belief is objectively true.

This approach makes chaos magic uniquely adaptable. It allows the practitioner to draw from many different traditions without needing to adhere to any one of them. A chaos magician may borrow symbols from Wicca, ritual structure from Thelema, meditation from Buddhism, and language from science fiction. The mix is not just allowed, but actively encouraged. The goal is to discover what produces real change in the practitioner's life.

Sigils are one of the most popular tools used in chaos magic. A sigil is a symbol created to represent a specific intent. The magician designs the sigil, often by condensing a phrase or desire into an abstract glyph. The sigil is then charged through emotional or energetic focus, often during meditation, trance, or orgasm. Once charged, the magician releases attachment to the outcome, allowing the unconscious mind to carry out the desire without interference.

Another key concept in chaos magic is gnosis. Gnosis refers to a heightened state of awareness in which the conscious mind is bypassed and the deeper mind becomes receptive to magical influence. This state can be achieved through many ritual methods, including dancing, chanting, drumming, intense focus, exhaustion, or sensory deprivation. In this altered state, the magician implants their intention or works their ritual with maximum effectiveness.

Chaos magic does not reject structure entirely, it just views structure as temporary and optional. Rituals, tools, and symbols are used when they are useful and discarded when they are not. There are no required pantheons, sacred texts, or secret initiations. The only real rule is that results matter. If something does not work, it is adjusted or replaced. This pragmatic mindset has made chaos magic appealing to those with scientific, psychological, or skeptical inclinations.

Because chaos magic challenges tradition, it can appear confrontational or irreverent. But beneath the surface, it demands a deep level of responsibility. Without external rules, the practitioner must become their own guide. This means facing their own illusions, fears, and inconsistencies. It means taking full ownership of the magical process and its consequences. In this way, it is a path that rewards creativity, discipline, and radical honesty.

Chaos magic is often practiced in private, with few external signs. It requires no robes, titles, or lineage. However, some practitioners enjoy crafting elaborate rituals or blending magical work with visual art, poetry, or performance. Others focus on inner transformation, using magical techniques to deprogram limiting beliefs, uncover personal truths, and shape their reality from the inside out.

Critics of chaos magic sometimes accuse it of being superficial or self-indulgent, but for many practitioners, it is a deeply transformative path. It strips away dogma and forces the magician to confront their own power. It offers freedom, but not comfort. In chaos magic, there is no external authority to blame or follow. There is only the self, the will, and the infinite possibility of the moment.

When things feel too chaotic or uncertain, chaos magic offers a way to engage with that uncertainty as a source of creative power. It teaches that magic is a process to be lived, rather than just studied. A chaos magician does not seek to master some ancient esoteric tradition. Instead, they seek to master their own mind and its ability to shape the world around them.

28

BLOOD MAGIC

B lood magic involves the use of blood in a ritual setting to deepen power, create strong energetic bonds, and signal serious intent. It is a more controversial form of magic, often misunderstood due to fear, taboo, or its association with sacrifice. Yet in many cultures, blood sacrifice has long been seen as sacred or devotional. It is the essence of life, a symbol of lineage, and a link between body and spirit.

In ancient times, blood was offered to the gods to seal pacts, honor the dead, or ask for protection. Across Mesopotamia, Egypt, Greece, Africa, and the Americas, blood was used to feed the spirits and awaken the land. In some traditions, it was used in rites of passage to mark birth, adulthood, or initiation. In others, it was poured into the earth as a gift to ancestors or spirits of place. These acts were not done lightly. They were solemn moments meant to create real change and lasting connection.

Modern blood magic does not involve violence or harm. Most practitioners use only a small drop of their own blood, drawn with care and intention. This is often done with a sterile lancet or pin, and only in a controlled, sacred setting. The use of blood in this way is symbolic. It says to the spirits, to the universe, and to the self: "I *am serious. I am willing to give of my own life force to see this work through.*"

Blood can be added to written spells, used to anoint candles or tools, or placed on a sigil to charge it with personal energy. Some use blood to seal oaths, strengthen bindings, or connect more deeply to a deity or familiar spirit. A few practitioners include it in potions or charms, but always with care, always in trace amounts, and always in accordance with safety and respect.

The power of blood lies in your identity. It carries your DNA, your memories, your pain, and your will. When added to your magical practice, it links the spell directly to you. It is like signing a contract in your own name. Because of this, blood magic is not used for casual desires or half-formed thoughts. It should be reserved only for protection, transformation, healing, and deep commitment.

There are certainly some ethical questions surrounding blood magic. Consent is always essential. Never use someone else's blood without their full and informed permission. Do not use animal blood unless you are following a cultural practice with full awareness, purpose, and reverence. Most importantly, never use blood to manipulate or harm others. The energy of blood magic is intense, and it carries serious consequences. It must *always* be approached with reverence.

Blood is also sacred in many feminine traditions, particularly those that honor the menstrual cycle. Some witches use menstrual blood in rituals to connect with their body, their ancestors, or the phases of the moon. It is not seen as unclean or shameful, but as a natural source of power. This practice is deeply personal and varies from person to person, but for many it becomes a way to reclaim spiritual authority and bodily wisdom.

There are also times when blood should *not* be used. If you are feeling physically or emotionally unstable, if you have an open wound or infection, or if you are unsure about your intentions, it is best to wait. You do not need blood to do powerful magic. It is just one tool among many, and its power ultimately comes from its symbolic representation of personal sacrifice.

Blood magic is not inherently dark. It is primal, bringing you closer to the edge of body and spirit. It is magic that asks something of *you* in return. It does not require fear, only respect. When used properly, it can help you express deep unwavering commitment in your rituals.

To practice blood magic is to say, this is mine. This is real. I claim this spell with every part of who I am. It is a way of weaving your literal biological essence into something magical. It is not a practice for everyone, and it should never be done lightly, but in the right hands, blood magic remains one of the most powerful forms of spiritual commitment known to mankind.

29

BANEFUL MAGIC

Baneful magic, often referred to as "black magic", is the use of magical practices intended to inflict pain, suffering, misfortune, or harm upon another living being. It is considered by many to be a path of evil, used to attack, retaliate, control, or punish a person or situation through spiritual means. This often includes the use of curses, hexes, bindings, and other forms of directed harm. While this chapter explores the origins and theory of baneful magic, I do not condone its use. The goal here is understanding, not instruction. Baneful magic exists in nearly every magical tradition, but its consequences are real and often damaging to everyone involved.

Baneful magic often arises when people feel powerless, violated, or desperate for justice. In some cultures, it has been used as a last resort when no earthly authority could be trusted to get the job done. In others, it has been woven into folklore, symbolizing the darker aspects of human will. But even when justified by anger or grief, baneful magic risks creating cycles of harm that entangle both caster and target. Just because something is possible does not mean it should be done.

This chapter is not meant to encourage the use of baneful spells.

It is written so that readers may understand these practices in context and make informed, ethical choices in their own spiritual path. Please keep this in mind as you continue reading.

Curses

A curse is a targeted working of magical energy intended to cause harm. It may bring illness, confusion, financial loss, emotional distress, or general misfortune. Some curses are designed to break relationships or influence behavior, while others are more abstract, simply wishing a general force of ruin on someone's life.

Historically, curses were found in ancient Egypt, Mesopotamia, Greece, and Rome. Lead tablets were inscribed with names and buried at crossroads or in graves. In some folk traditions, items were used such as dolls, hair, and pins, buried or burned as a focus for harmful intent. Curses have appeared in both individual practices and entire systems of magical justice, including those of certain African diaspora religions, where a clear moral structure governed the use of such work.

Modern curses may take the form of written spells, spoken declarations, crafted objects, or mental visualizations. They often involve symbolic ingredients such as thorns, nails, graveyard soil, or fire. Some use the name or belongings of the target to form a link. Whether elaborate or simple, the purpose unfortunately remains the same: to cause harm.

It is important to understand that curses carry weight. Even when justified, they tie the practitioner to the emotional and energetic state of the situation. Many traditions believe that a curse can echo back on the caster if not properly grounded, released, and shielded. For this reason alone, many practitioners choose never to curse, and instead redirect harmful energy or protect themselves through nonviolent means.

Bindings

A binding is a form of baneful or neutral magic that seeks to restrict someone's power rather than cause direct harm. A binding may be used to stop someone from spreading lies, committing abuse, or continuing a pattern of harm. In some cases, it is an act of protection rather than vengeance.

Binding spells often involve string, knots, wax, or symbolic containment. The goal is to limit a person's influence or halt their actions. This might include writing a name on paper, wrapping it tightly, and sealing it in a jar or box. Some use clay or poppets to represent the target and physically restrict them. Others perform visualizations where they imagine the person held in stasis or surrounded by mirrors that reflect their actions back at them.

Even if not aggressive, bindings are still a form of control and should be approached with caution. Ask yourself if the binding is truly necessary or if other solutions are available. If used at all, a binding should be released once its purpose is fulfilled.

Demonology

Demonology refers to the study of spirits that have traditionally been labeled as demons. In Western occult systems, these beings are often seen not as evil forces, but as powerful entities of transformation and hidden knowledge. Some magical grimoires, such as the *Ars Goetia,* contain instructions for summoning and commanding such spirits, often through complex rituals and sacred names.

In baneful magic, demons may be invoked to punish, attack, or spiritually confront a person or situation. Practitioners may request a demon's help in revealing secrets, causing misfortune, or protecting themselves through fear and intimidation.

The dangers of this work are many. Demonology is not for beginners, and it should not be used as a tool for revenge. These spirits do not operate by human morality and can not be approached casually.

Whether you believe they are real beings or just psychological archetypes, demons evoke deep unconscious forces that can overwhelm those who are unprepared. Working with such spirits requires boundaries, precision, and respect, or the cost may be far greater than the result.

The Law of Return

Every magical act creates an energetic echo. When you send harm into the world, it will return in unexpected ways. Some religious traditions call this karma. Practitioners of magic call it the Law of Return. When you curse, bind, or summon spirits in anger, you invite those forces into your energy field. Even if you succeed in harming your target, you may carry the residue of that act long after it is finished.

Common consequences include persistent anger, paranoia, fatigue, nightmares, and emotional imbalance. Some practitioners also report hauntings, reversed luck, or entanglement with the person they sought to harm. The more intense the emotional charge, the deeper the imprint it can leave on your energy and your environment.

For this reason, many witches, healers, and energy workers recommend transmutation instead of attack. Transform your pain into protection. Transform your grief into clarity. Redirect rather than retaliate. Defend yourself, yes, but do not become a mirror of the harm you once received.

Baneful magic is part of the magical world, but it should never be the default choice. If you are tempted to curse, ask yourself why. Have you explored other options? Have you spoken your truth, set boundaries, or removed yourself from harm? Have you worked on healing your own pain?

There is power in refusal. To be able to "just walk away" is a sign of strength, not defeat. If you choose *not* to use baneful magic, you lose nothing, all while remaining in alignment with your own values.

Instead, focus your energy on building rather than breaking. This way, you become a channel for healing, rather than destruction. This path does not mean you are weak, it means you are awake. You know what you are capable of, and you choose to wield that power with care.

30

NECROMANCY

Necromancy is the practice of communicating with the dead. The term comes from ancient Greek, where "nekros" means dead and "manteia" means divination. Contrary to many modern depictions, necromancy is not solely concerned with raising corpses or controlling the undead. Its true purpose is to seek guidance, knowledge, or power from the spirits of those who have passed.

In ancient cultures, necromancy was practiced as a sacred rite. In Mesopotamia, Greece, and Rome, rituals were performed to consult the dead through dreams, visions, or offerings. Graveyards especially were seen as places of power where the boundaries between the worlds were thinner. Shamans and oracles would seek out these places to ask questions of the ancestors or commune with shades for prophecy. In some traditions, necromancers were revered as spiritual intermediaries who could resolve family curses, uncover hidden knowledge, or guide souls to peace.

The practice of necromancy often involves tools and rites intended to open communication with the spirit world. This may include the use of candles, bones, graveyard dirt, spirit boards, mirrors, or ancestral objects. The practitioner must prepare a sacred space with protection in mind, as working with the dead requires reverence and care. Offerings such as wine, bread, flowers, or coins may be left at graves or altars. Prayers and invocations are spoken to call forth the spirit or to ask for its presence in dreams or meditation.

Necromancy is not inherently dangerous, but it must be approached with ethical grounding. The dead are not to be disturbed for frivolous or selfish reasons. Consent is vital. One does not demand answers from spirits, but requests them. Many necromancers develop relationships with specific ancestors or spirit allies who serve as guides or protectors in their work. These relationships grow over time and form the core of safe and effective practice.

Modern necromancy often focuses on ancestor work. Many witches and spiritual practitioners build ancestral altars where they leave offerings and communicate through dreams, writing, or divination. Ancestors may be called upon for healing, insight, protection, or the resolution of unfinished family patterns. This work helps to restore connection across generations and honors the lineage one comes from.

Another aspect of necromancy involves psychopomp work. A psychopomp is a spiritual guide who helps souls transition from this world to the next. In some traditions, the practitioner may be called to assist wandering or restless spirits in finding peace. This can involve rituals of release, blessings, or guiding the spirit toward light. This form of necromancy is rooted in compassion and service.

Some forms of necromantic magic involve channeling messages from the dead through psychic mediumship or automatic writing. Others rely on traditional divination tools such as bones or cards charged with ancestral energy. Some even seek visions through trance or dreams, using mugwort or other herbs to enhance spiritual perception.

Working with the dead requires grounding and protection. Practitioners often cast circles, carry protective charms, or cleanse themselves after spirit work. Regular spiritual hygiene is important to avoid uninvited attachments or exhaustion. When performed with careful intention, necromancy can be a powerful form of healing and remembrance.

Séances

Séances are structured gatherings in which a group of people attempts to communicate with spirits. The word séance means "session" or "sitting" in French and became popular in the nineteenth century during the rise of spiritualism in Europe and America. The practice gained momentum with the work of famous mediums and the use of spirit boards, automatic writing, and table tipping.

Many séances were held in private homes or parlors, sometimes in near darkness, with participants joining hands to create a circle of unified intent. Candles were lit, prayers spoken, and a medium would enter a trance state to receive messages from spirits. Reports of knocking, cold spots, disembodied voices, and levitations were common. A well-led séance includes opening and closing rituals, cleansing of the space, and clear boundaries to protect participants from unwanted energies.

While some séances were genuine attempts to contact loved ones, others were fraudulent performances, leading to widespread skepticism. Despite this, many practitioners today continue to use séances in a sacred way, creating safe spaces for spirit communication and healing.

Exorcisms

Exorcisms are rituals designed to remove malevolent or unwanted spiritual entities from a person, place, or object. The practice has existed across many cultures for thousands of years. In ancient Babylon, priests performed incantations to drive out demons. In Judaism, rituals were developed to cleanse spiritual impurities. The Christian tradition popularized the image of the exorcist through the Gospels, where Jesus is described as casting out spirits. Catholic exorcisms became formalized, with prescribed rites involving holy water, sacred names, and intense prayer.

In magical practice, exorcism may include the use of salt, bells, incense, protective talismans, and invocation of spirit allies or deities. The goal is not to punish or destroy, but to restore harmony and assert spiritual authority over baneful spirits. Folk exorcists may use sweeping rituals, chanting, sacred smoke, and symbols drawn at thresholds. In some ways, it becomes a form of healing magic, as you are essentially cleansing the body of unwanted influence.

Successful exorcism requires strength of will, clarity of purpose, and deep respect for the power of the spirit world. Because of the emotional and spiritual strain involved, exorcisms should be approached with preparation, support, and caution. They are not to be undertaken lightly, and should only be used as a last resort for major disturbances in your life.

SECTION IV:
FOLK TRADITIONS

"Tradition is not the worship of ashes, but the preservation of fire."

— Gustav Mahler

31

SHAMANISM

S hamanism is the spiritual practice of engaging directly with the spirit world for healing, vision, and wisdom. At its core, it is the art of traveling between the physical and nonphysical realms to bring back knowledge or power that serves the well-being of the individual or the community. Unlike institutional religion, shamanism is experiential, fluid, and rooted in the natural cycles of the earth. It does not rely on belief, but on direct revelation through altered states of consciousness.

The word "shaman" comes from the Evenki people of Siberia, but the practices associated with it exist in many cultures around the world. These include the medicine people of the Americas, the spirit mediums of West Africa, the curanderos of Central America, the kahuna of Hawaii, and the dreamwalkers of Aboriginal Australia. Though their names, symbols, and myths differ, these traditions share foundational principles, especially their views on animism.

In most shamanic cultures, illness is not seen solely as a physical problem. It may be the result of soul loss, spiritual intrusion, broken taboos, or disharmony between a person and their environment. The shaman serves as a mediator, locating the root of the disorder through ritual, vision, or communication with helping spirits. In this sense, the shaman is not a magician who imposes will upon reality, but a guide who restores sacred connection between people, nature, and unseen realms.

The calling to become a shaman is often involuntary. It may come through a near-death experience, a sudden illness, or an intense period of psychological disintegration. In traditional cultures, these experiences are recognized as initiatory events, where the individual is dying to their old self and being reborn with a spiritual mandate. This crisis may involve visions, dreams, or encounters with spirits who demand the person step into their role. Without this transformation, the person may remain unwell. With it, they are reborn with new insight and gifts.

The primary method of shamanic work is the spirit journey. This is not metaphorical. The shaman shifts consciousness to travel into invisible realms, often categorized as the lower world, middle world, and upper world. These are not places in the sky or beneath the ground, but subtle dimensions of spiritual reality. The lower world is home to ancestral energies, animal spirits, and primal wisdom. The upper world contains celestial teachers and beings of great light. The middle world reflects the soul of the present world and includes both helpful and harmful spirits. Shamans journey between these worlds in pursuit of healing, divination, or the recovery of ancestral power.

Drumming, rattling, dancing, and breathwork are common techniques to induce the trance state. The steady beat of a drum, especially around four to seven beats per second, synchronizes with the theta brainwave state. This opens the doorway to visionary experience. Once in trance, the shaman does not control the journey, but rather surrenders to it. They follow signs, images, and spiritual guides that appear to them and interpret what they are shown upon returning.

Power animals or spirit allies often accompany the shaman. These are not symbols or imagined figures. They are autonomous beings who teach, protect, and guide. A person might discover their power animal through a vision, a dream, or a journey guided by a more experienced practitioner. This ally may stay for life or change over time. Working with power animals builds confidence, deepens spiritual protection, and reminds the practitioner that they are not walking alone.

Healing in shamanism is holistic. It may involve soul retrieval, where lost fragments of a person's essence are found and returned. These fragments are usually lost during trauma, especially events that cause fear, betrayal, grief, or shock. When soul loss occurs, people may feel numb, disconnected, chronically fatigued, or unable to move forward. In a soul retrieval, the shaman brings back the missing part and reintegrates it through ritual and care.

Another form of healing is extraction. This is the removal of intrusive energies or spiritual blockages that do not belong to the person's natural field. These might be thought forms, entities, curses, or psychic residue left from difficult relationships or environments. The shaman identifies the source of disturbance and removes it using energetic tools, helping the body and soul return to harmony.

Some shamans also work with ancestral spirits and the dead. In cultures where the line between the living and the departed is thin, shamans help the dead cross over, resolve unfinished business, or deliver messages to the living. In other cases, ancestral patterns may be affecting a person's present life. The shaman helps heal these patterns so that future generations are not burdened by them.

In many traditions, nature itself is the greatest teacher. Trees, rivers, stones, animals, and winds are not inanimate objects but living, speaking beings. A shaman may go into the forest, the desert, or the mountains to commune with these spirits, asking for insight or healing. Rituals might include burying offerings, fasting, creating sacred fires, or constructing altars from natural materials. The land becomes a teacher, and every experience becomes part of the learning. In this way, shamanism is deeply tied to the concept of animism, which we have explored in earlier chapters.

In modern times, shamanism has experienced a revival. People around the world are returning to earth-centered spirituality, seeking ways to reconnect with their intuition and the sacredness of life. Contemporary shamanic practitioners adapt the core methods of journeying, energy work, and spiritual healing without imitating specific indigenous cultures. This approach, often called core shamanism, focuses on universal techniques that honor the essence of the practice while respecting cultural boundaries.

There are also modern practitioners who study directly with indigenous teachers, integrating traditional knowledge with humility and permission. Ethical shamanic practice today requires awareness of cultural appropriation, as well as deep respect for the sacred. It is not a title to be claimed lightly. True shamanic work is a lifelong path of service, not a trend or tool for personal gain.

You do not need to become a shaman to benefit from shamanic wisdom. You can learn to journey, connect with nature spirits, honor your ancestors, and bring sacred presence into your life. You can enter altered states through drumming or breath, work with your dreams, and listen to what the land has to say. Shamanism teaches us to trust what we feel in our hearts. It reminds us that healing is not only about the body, but also the soul. That wisdom does not come only from books, but from trees, stars, and silence. The world is alive with spirit, just waiting for us to remember how to speak its language.

VOODOO & HOODOO

V oodoo is a sacred spiritual tradition that blends West African religion with Indigenous practices and Catholicism. It developed through the survival and resilience of enslaved Africans who brought their beliefs with them to the Americas. In places like Haiti, New Orleans, and parts of the Caribbean and South America, these traditions evolved into unique systems of worship rooted in ancestry, nature, and spirit.

Though the word Voodoo is often misused in popular culture, its true form is a deeply devotional and complex religion. It is not a system of spells or superstition, but a path of healing, service, and sacred relationship. Practitioners of Voodoo work closely with the spirits, ancestors, and natural forces, guided by ritual, music, and community connection.

The foundation of Voodoo rests on the worship of a supreme creator, often referred to as Bondye. However, Bondye is considered distant and not directly involved in daily life. Instead, Voodoo practitioners serve spirits, known as loa, that act as a sort of spiritual medium to Bondye. This is very similar to the way Catholics will ask saints to pray to god on their behalf. Each loa governs different aspects of life such as love, justice, fertility, war, and healing. The loa are not worshipped but honored through offerings, song, dance, and ritual possession to ultimately gain favor with Bondye.

In a Voodoo ceremony, a priest or priestess may call upon the loa by drawing a veve, which is a symbolic sigil made of cornmeal or flour. This opens a gateway for the spirit to enter the space. Music, drumming, and dance are essential parts of the ritual. As the ceremony unfolds, a loa may choose to mount or possess a participant, speaking and acting through them. This experience may sound frightening, but to practitioners it is a sacred moment of deep connection between the spirit world and the human one.

Ancestral reverence is another core pillar of Voodoo. Ancestors are considered part of the spiritual family, and they are honored regularly through prayers, offerings, and altar work. The presence of ancestors is felt in daily life, and their wisdom and protection are sought in times of need. Death is not the end in Voodoo, but a continuation of the soul's journey through the spirit world.

Haitian Vodou, Louisiana Voodoo, and West African Vodun all have shared roots, but distinct expressions of the practice. Haitian Vodou is highly organized and ritualistic, guided by initiatory lineages and formal ceremonies. Louisiana Voodoo, while deeply spiritual, developed under conditions of secrecy and oppression, and often incorporates rootwork, candle magic, and personal charms. West African Vodun remains closest to its original form, with complex systems of gods, sacred drumming, and community ritual.

Despite centuries of colonial suppression and cultural misrepresentation, Voodoo has endured. It is not a dark or dangerous religion. Its focus is on healing, justice, relationship, and survival. Many practitioners pursue Voodoo after feeling a deep ancestral pull or a calling from the spirits. While Voodoo includes workings for protection and spiritual defense, the idea that it is a religion of curses is both false and harmful.

The spirits of Voodoo are thought to be omnipresent, laced within the fabric of reality itself. They exist in rivers, trees, crossroads, fire, and wind. They speak through dreams, intuition, and ritual. Serving the spirits is not about personal gain. It is about balance, responsibility, and community. Each loa has their own likes and dislikes, colors, songs, and symbols. To work with them requires knowledge and respect.

Initiation is a serious and lifelong commitment in Voodoo. Those who wish to be initiated must seek a legitimate priest or priestess, train under their guidance, and be accepted by the spirits. This process is not meant for the curious or casual. It is a sacred responsibility passed through generations, and in some branches of Voodoo, completely closed off to outsiders.

Despite its somewhat rigid initiatory structure, Voodoo can still be quite practical. Healing ceremonies, herbal medicine, spiritual baths, and divination are all part of everyday practice. Illness is seen as both physical and spiritual. A person may be cleansed with herbs and smoke, prayed over, or bathed in sacred waters to restore harmony. Divination helps reveal hidden truths and guides decisions. Offerings to the spirits might include rum, cigars, coins, flowers, food, or sacred objects that are meaningful to the loa.

Practitioners often maintain personal altars. These spaces are decorated with candles, photos of ancestors, sacred objects, and statues of spirits. They serve as a point of daily connection to the unseen world. A practitioner may light a candle each morning, offer a cup of coffee to an ancestor, or sing to a spirit to keep the relationship alive.

It is important for outsiders to understand that Voodoo is not a magical system to be copied or used without context. It is a religion. To approach it with sincerity, one must study its history, respect its elders, and engage in it as a living tradition. Misappropriation and misunderstanding have already caused deep harm, and it is essential that Voodoo be honored for what it truly is.

Even today, Voodoo continues to grow and evolve. In Haiti, it remains a national religion practiced by millions. In New Orleans, it is tied to the city's cultural and spiritual heritage. Across the world, people are reconnecting with their ancestral traditions through Voodoo. It offers strength, healing, protection, and deep connection to the land and its spirits.

Poppets

Poppets are small human-shaped figures used in voodoo to represent a person for the purpose of healing, blessing, protection, or other forms of magical focus. These figures may be made from cloth, wax, corn husks, clay, or natural materials such as sticks and roots. Though commonly associated with superstition and baneful intent in popular media, poppets are most often used for benevolent and healing purposes.

In many folk traditions, including those influenced by Voodoo, poppets serve as a symbolic link to an individual. This connection allows the practitioner to direct energy toward that person through ritual. A poppet may be created to help someone recover from illness, to carry their prayers, to shield them from harm, or to draw love and abundance into their life.

The process of making a poppet is both spiritual and intentional. The figure is crafted by hand and often filled or decorated with personal items such as hair, nail clippings, bits of clothing, photos, or handwritten notes. Herbs, stones, and charms are added to align the poppet with the desired outcome. Lavender and rose petals may be used for peace and love, while salt, rosemary, or iron filings might be used for protection.

Once the poppet is complete, it is named and spoken to as if it were the person it represents. Prayers are said over it, candles may be lit beside it, and offerings may be given in its honor. The poppet may be kept on an altar, carried in a charm bag, or used in ritual acts such as anointing, binding, or burial to symbolize spiritual change or completion.

Poppets are effective not because of their material, but because of the intention and relationship behind their creation. They act as a physical stand-in for spiritual focus, allowing the practitioner to direct energy with clarity and care. Rooted in the principle of sympathetic magic, a well-crafted poppet becomes a conduit for healing, transformation, and protection. When made with proper intent, it reflects the heart of folk magic: that attention, intention, and connection are what make a spell work.

Hoodoo

Hoodoo is a tradition of African American folk magic that developed in the southern United States. It draws from African spirituality, Indigenous practices, biblical imagery, and European folklore. Unlike Voodoo, which is a religion, Hoodoo is a system of practical magic focused on survival, protection, luck, and justice. It is not an organized religion but a folk tradition passed down through families and communities.

Hoodoo includes the use of candle work, rootwork, prayer, and personal rituals. It often incorporates psalms, spiritual baths, floor washes, and the creation of charms and mojo bags. These practices are meant to bring about real-world results, like success in relationships or financial abundance. Hoodoo is deeply tied to the lived experiences of Black Americans and has long served as a form of resistance, empowerment, and ancestral continuity for them.

Conjure

Conjure is often used interchangeably with Hoodoo but can refer more broadly to the act of calling in spiritual forces to achieve a result. A conjure worker may call on the spirits of ancestors, saints, or personal guides for help. The term also emphasizes the spoken word, prayer, and charm as key tools in the work. Conjure is personal and adaptive. It is shaped by the practitioner's heritage, relationship to spirit, and intention.

Conjure also includes spiritual diagnosis and cleansing. A root doctor or conjure woman may read signs in candle wax, dreams, or nature, then prescribe a course of spiritual treatment. This could involve herbs, oil dressings, baths, or amulets. The aim is to bring harmony between the spiritual and physical body.

Rootwork

Rootwork refers specifically to the use of herbs, roots, minerals, and curios in magical practice. It is the botanical heart of Hoodoo. Each root or plant has specific properties and is used in spells, gris-gris bags, powders, or oils. For example, High John the Conqueror root is associated with strength and overcoming adversity. Devil's Shoe String is used for protection and luck. These materials are often combined with ritual gestures, prayer, and timing to create powerful workings.

Rootworkers often maintain apothecaries of dried herbs, oils, roots, and stones. They may create custom spell kits, anointing oils, or spiritual candles. Rootwork is direct, grounded, and focused on tangible results. It is an accessible form of folk magic that connects the practitioner with nature, spirit, and tradition.

SANTERÍA & CURANDERISMO

Among the many paths of folk magic, few are as culturally rich and spiritually complex as the traditions of Santería and Curanderismo. Rooted in Latin America and the Caribbean, these systems reflect centuries of spiritual survival, blending Indigenous knowledge, Catholic iconography, and African cosmologies. Beyond just a magical practice, they are living traditions of healing, resistance, and devotion for these communities.

While both Santería and Curanderismo involve interaction with the unseen world, they arise from distinct cultural lineages and serve different spiritual roles. Curanderismo is a path of healing, rooted in the land and the body. Santería, also known as *La Regla de Ocha*, is a full-fledged Afro-Caribbean religion with its own pantheon, priesthood, and rituals. Together, they reveal the depth and diversity of spiritual life across Latin America and the diaspora.

Many practitioners today are reconnecting with these traditions after generations of silence or separation. Colonial violence, religious suppression, and cultural erasure have long interrupted the transmission of this knowledge. As interest in ancestral traditions grows, more people are returning to the spiritual systems that once guided their families and communities.

Contrary to how they are often portrayed in media or pop culture, these traditions rarely incorporate baneful magic and their work exists within a complex moral landscape. Curanderismo emphasizes healing, service, and the restoration of harmony. Santería emphasizes maintaining good relationships with the orishas, the natural world, and the spiritual obligations one carries. Neither tradition is reducible to binary notions of good or evil. Both require respect for spiritual forces, personal accountability, and the wisdom to navigate life's challenges with clarity and care. Let's explore both in more detail to better understand how they differ.

Santería

Santería, also known as *La Regla de Ocha*, is a syncretic Afro-Caribbean religion that emerged in Cuba among enslaved Yoruba people who were forced to conceal their spiritual practices under Catholic imagery. It weaves together West African Orisha worship, Catholic saint veneration, and elements of spiritism and folk magic.

At the heart of Santería is a complex relationship with the orishas; divine beings who embody forces of nature and aspects of human experience. Practitioners build personal relationships with these orishas through offerings, songs, drumming, and initiation. Each orisha has distinct colors, attributes, preferences, and domains, from the fiery justice of Changó, to the nurturing wisdom of Yemayá, and the crossroads mastery of Eleguá.

Rituals in Santería are communal and ceremonial. Divination with tools like diloggun (cowrie shells) or obi (coconut) is used to communicate with the orishas and seek guidance. Initiation rites are deeply sacred and involve years of preparation, commitment, and spiritual rebirth.

Santería is not a system of casual spellwork, it is a religion grounded in reciprocity, lineage, and spiritual discipline. Practitioners are expected to live in harmony with the guidance of the orishas and honor the natural cycles of life and death. Ancestors play a central role, and their veneration is often integrated into household altars and daily prayers.

Despite long histories of persecution, misrepresentation, and exoticization, Santería remains a powerful, affirming path for many across the Afro-Latinx diaspora. It offers community, identity, and a profound sense of belonging in a world that often seeks to erase or marginalize these traditional ways.

Curanderismo

Curanderismo is a traditional healing system practiced across Mexico, Central America, South America, and the American Southwest. A curandero or curandera is a healer of the body *and* soul, often called upon for emotional pain, spiritual blockages, and disharmony in a person's life. In fact, it is not uncommon for real functional medicine doctors to practice elements of curanderismo in order to give their patients more holistic care.

This path sees health as the result of balance: between body and spirit, between the individual and the community, between humans and nature. When illness appears, it is often understood as a sign of deeper misalignment that must be addressed through both physical and spiritual means.

The practice includes herbal remedies, spiritual cleansings, energy work, massage, and prayer. A hallmark ritual is the limpia: a cleansing ceremony that uses eggs, herbs, or flowers to draw out negative energy. Afterward, the egg may be cracked into water and interpreted for insight, revealing hidden emotional wounds or spiritual disturbances.

Though curanderismo often incorporates Catholic imagery, such as prayers to saints, the use of holy water, or devotion to the Virgin, it operates outside the confines of formal religion. It blends ancient plant wisdom with spiritual intuition, serving as a bridge between worlds. Curanderos are often guides, mentors, and community elders. They support people in times of grief, transition, and uncertainty, offering remedies and spiritual counsel. In this way, curanderismo continues to be a vital thread in the spiritual fabric of many Latin communities.

34

THE FAE

The fae are nature spirits, sometimes called the fair folk, who are believed in European Folk magic to dwell in the hidden spaces of the natural world. These beings are not small winged creatures from children's stories but powerful, mysterious, and sometimes unpredictable forces of the land. In traditional European folklore, fae spirits are known to inhabit forests, rivers, mountains, meadows, and even household hearths. They are thought to exist between the human world and the spirit world and be deeply connected to the cycles of nature.

The word "fae" comes from old French and Latin roots, meaning enchantment or fate. Across Europe and other parts of the world, fae-like beings appear in myth and legend under many names. In Ireland and Scotland they are called the *aos sí* or the *daoine sídhe*. In Scandinavia they are the *huldufólk* or "hidden people." In Slavic countries they are the *domovoi* and *leshy*. In these traditions, the fae are more mischievous than whimsical. They are ancient spirits who demand respect and caution.

Unlike other spirits who may be summoned or directed, the fae are autonomous and have their own rules. They are bound to the land and its cycles, often appearing or withdrawing with the seasons.

Some may choose to work with humans while others prefer to remain hidden. To practice fae magic is to honor their presence, learn their customs, and approach them with humility, as if they are a real presence in the land.

The best way to begin working with the fae is through observation. Spend time in natural places where their presence is strong. These include old forests, wild gardens, standing stones, springs, and crossroads. Approach these places with quiet reverence. Listen more than you speak. Leave offerings such as milk, honey, bread, or shiny objects as a sign of goodwill. Never take anything from their space without asking first. Never assume their help or try to command them. Working with the fae is about relationship, not control.

Fae spirits have been known to offer blessings to those they favor. These blessings can come in the form of intuition, healing, artistic inspiration, protection, or assistance in magical work. However, they are just as capable of trickery or punishment when disrespected. Folklore is filled with warnings about breaking promises to the fae or crossing into their territory without invitation. The line between gift and curse is often thin, and caution is always required.

Fae magic often overlaps with the natural magic of plants, stones, animals, and weather. There are several herbs associated with the fae including foxglove, elder, hawthorn, and rowan. These plants are sometimes considered gateways or wards for the fae to enter our realm, so they should be handled with care. Circles of mushrooms, known as fairy rings, are traditionally seen as portals between worlds. Entering such a ring without permission is thought to cause confusion, time loss, or even being taken into the otherworld.

The otherworld is the realm where the fae are said to live. It exists parallel to our own, accessible through dreams, sacred sites, or moments of liminality. Dawn, dusk, and twilight are especially powerful times for fae contact. The solstices, equinoxes, and the cross-quarter days, like Beltane and Samhain, are also considered times when the veil between the worlds is thin and communication becomes easier.

In working with the fae, it is important to practice spiritual cleanliness and grounding. Fae energy can be disorienting or intoxicating. Carrying iron is traditionally said to repel harmful fae but may also offend helpful ones. Some practitioners use protective charms, wear silver jewelry, or keep a piece of rowan or salt with them when doing fae work. Trust your intuition and know when to engage and when to step back.

Modern fae practitioners often blend folk traditions with personal experience. Some keep faery altars with natural objects, others write poems or songs as offerings. Some journey in meditation to the otherworld to meet with guides and guardians. Dreams, omens, and sudden shifts in emotion or weather are all seen as possible signs of fae contact. Pay attention to animals acting strangely, lights flickering, or finding gifts like feathers and stones in unexpected places.

Approaching fae magic means remembering that you are not the center of the story. You are a guest on sacred land. The fae will test your intentions, watch how you treat the forest, and respond accordingly. They reward those who are kind, creative, and truthful. They avoid those who are greedy, careless, or arrogant. Their magic is a mirror, reflecting any energy you bring to it.

In a time when the natural world is actively being ignored or abused, fae magic offers a way to rekindle our ancestral love for nature. It reminds us that nature is alive with spirit, and that magic is hidden all around us. If we pay close enough attention, that hidden world will reveal itself to us.

CONCLUSION
FINDING YOUR PATH

Spirituality is not a destination you arrive at, but a path you walk. It twists, it climbs, it pauses, and sometimes it loops back on itself. It is not a ladder with steps to ascend but a forest with many trails, each one shaped by your experiences. This book has walked you through many such trails. You have explored ancient traditions, elemental energies, esoteric systems, and the intimate magic of everyday life. Now it is time to turn inward and ask the most important question of all. What is *your* path?

The search for spirituality is not about finding the most powerful rituals or memorizing the most complex doctrines. It is about uncovering the practices that speak to your soul. Some will feel familiar, as if you are remembering something you once knew. Others may challenge your beliefs and invite you to grow. Every system you have read about has something to teach, even if it is not meant to be your destination. It is okay to be drawn to many things at once. Curiosity is not confusion. It is a sign that your spirit is awake.

There is no right way to walk the spiritual path. Some people begin with meditation and slowly move into magic. Others avoid spellwork and only seek philosophical depth. Some build altars.

Others wander the woods. Some call themselves witches, pagans, mystics, or animists. Others reject all labels. What matters is not what you call yourself, but how you carry yourself throughout daily life. What values are most important to you? Do your practices bring you closer to truth? Do they nourish your heart? Do they remind you that you are part of something greater?

The journey is not always easy. At times, you may feel lost. At times, you may doubt what you believe. You may even go through periods of silence where nothing speaks to you. This is part of the path too. Growth often happens in the quiet. Do not be afraid to set things down when they no longer serve you. Let your path evolve and surprise you. Let it reflect the seasons of your life. Consistent spiritual growth comes from a willingness to keep listening.

You may find that your path is not just about *what* you practice, but *how* you practice. Some people need structure, routine, and ceremony. Others thrive in fluid, intuitive exploration. Neither is better. Your path should fit you like a second skin, not a tight costume. Allow your practice to honor your rhythms, your mental state, your energy levels, and your unique needs. Spirituality is not meant to be another source of pressure. It is meant to be a source of renewal.

As you move forward, you might feel called to create your own path from the pieces that resonate with you most. This is not a sign of failure or indecision. Traditions are not fixed. They evolve through people who dare to engage with them authentically. You have permission to be one of those people. You have permission to blend, to adapt, to question, and to create.

Trust your instincts. Keep a journal. Pay attention to signs, symbols, and synchronicities. Be open to mentorship and community, but never give your power away. Learn from others, but return often to your own center. That is where your compass lives. The deeper you go within yourself, the more clearly you will hear the voice of your path calling to you.

Your spiritual life is not something you must master or prove. It will change as you change, and deepen as you deepen. Whether you practice magic daily or only when the moment calls for it, whether you identify with a specific tradition or carve your own, your path is sacred because it is yours. Take what resonates. Leave what does not. Keep walking. The path is always unfolding.

GLOSSARY

Alchemy: A spiritual and symbolic science focused on transformation, both of the self and of matter; often expressed through metaphors of turning base metals into gold.

Altar: A sacred surface or space used in rituals to hold tools, offerings, or symbols of devotion.

Amulet: An object worn or carried for magical protection or luck, often charged with specific intentions.

Animism: The belief that all natural things (plants, rocks, rivers, even manmade objects) possess a spiritual essence or consciousness.

Astral Projection: The practice of intentionally leaving the physical body in spirit to explore other realms or planes of existence.

Athame: A ritual dagger used in many magical traditions to direct energy, not for physical cutting.

Baneful Magic: Magic intended to cause harm, limit, or punish, often raising ethical concerns for the practitioner.

Binding: A magical act intended to limit someone's influence or actions, typically for protective purposes.

Besom: A broom used in ritual, especially for energetically sweeping or purifying a space.

Blood Magic: The use of blood in spellwork as a potent personal offering or binding force.

Book of Shadows: A magical record or journal containing spells, rituals, correspondences, and personal reflections.

Cauldron: A small cast-iron pot, often used in witchcraft, divination, or herbal brews.

Candles: Used in spellwork to invoke spirits or the element of fire; represents intention, timing, or deity presence.

Ceremonial Magic: A structured form of magic involving complex rituals, sacred geometry, and invocation of spiritual beings or cosmic forces.

Chakras: Seven primary energy centers located along the spine, each associated with physical, emotional, and spiritual functions.

Chaos Magic: A modern magical paradigm that values belief as a tool and emphasizes experimentation over tradition.

Chalice: A ritual cup representing the element of water, commonly used in Wiccan and ceremonial rites.

Conjure: A folk magic practice, especially in Hoodoo, involving prayer, spoken spells, and physical tools to influence events.

Correspondences: Symbolic associations. such as colors, herbs, planets, and days of the week, used to align magical tools with intent.

Crystals: Stones believed to carry energetic properties that support healing, protection, or spiritual focus.

Dandelion: A plant used in folk magic for wish-making, psychic opening, and spirit communication.

Divination: The practice of gaining insight or guidance through symbolic tools like tarot, runes, pendulums, or scrying.

Dreamwork: The exploration of dreams for healing, symbolism, or contact with spirit realms.

Elements: The five foundational energies of Earth, Air, Fire, Water, and Spirit that underlie most magical philosophy.

Energy: The unseen life force that flows through all things; the basis of most magical practices.

Etheric Body: A subtle energetic layer of the human aura, thought to be closely connected to the physical body.

Fae: Nature spirits or supernatural beings from European folklore, often mischievous and bound by their own magical laws.

Folk Magic: Practical, community-rooted magic passed through oral traditions, often tied to survival, healing, and local spirits.

Golden Dawn: A 19th-century occult order that influenced modern ceremonial magic, known for its complex rituals and use of Kabbalah.

Grimoire: A magical textbook or journal of rituals, spells, correspondences, and personal discoveries.

Green Witch: A practitioner who focuses on plant-based magic, herbalism, and communion with nature spirits.

Healing Magic: Spellwork and ritual intended to restore physical, emotional, or spiritual well-being.

Herbs: Plants used in magic and healing for their symbolic and energetic qualities.

Hoodoo: An African American folk magic system combining Christian prayer, herbal medicine, rootwork, and ancestral knowledge.

Hex: A curse placed on someone, typically intended to harm or hinder.

Incense: Burned aromatic substances used to purify space, invoke spirits, or align with specific magical goals.

Intention: The directed purpose or focus behind any magical act; the energetic engine of spellwork.

Karma: A concept from Eastern traditions that suggests spiritual cause and effect; every action carries a consequence, seen or unseen.

Lucid Dreaming: The state of being aware within a dream, often allowing the dreamer to control or influence the dream world.

Lesser Banishing Ritual of the Pentagram (LBRP): A protective ceremonial ritual used to clear negative energy and invoke elemental balance.

Magic: The art of intentionally working with unseen forces to influence reality; often defined as "the science and art of causing change in conformity with will."

Mojo Bag: A small charm bag used in Hoodoo, filled with herbs, roots, coins, or personal items for protection, love, luck, or power.

Monotheism: The belief in a singular, all-powerful god; contrasted in the book with polytheistic and animist views.

Mugwort: An herb traditionally used for psychic opening, dreamwork, and spirit contact.

Necromancy: The practice of communing with the dead for guidance, knowledge, or magical aid.

Nature Magic: Magic rooted in the rhythms of the earth, seasons, moon phases, and living ecosystems.

Paganism: A broad term for earth-based, polytheistic, and often revivalist spiritual paths honoring gods, nature, and seasonal cycles.

Past Life Regression: A meditative or hypnotic technique used to recall alleged previous incarnations.

Pentacle: A five-pointed star within a circle, symbolizing the elements in balance; a protective emblem in many magical traditions.

Poppet: A doll used in sympathetic magic to represent a person for healing, binding, or influence.

Protection Magic: Spells, amulets, rituals, and wards designed to shield oneself or others from harm or negativity.

Ritual: A repeated sequence of actions performed with spiritual or magical intent, often aligned with timing or cosmic forces.

Rootwork: The botanical practice within Hoodoo of using roots, herbs, and minerals in spellwork and conjure.

Runes: Ancient symbols used in Norse divination and magical inscriptions.

Santería: A syncretic Afro-Caribbean religion combining Yoruba deities (Orishas) with Catholic saint worship and ritual.

Scrying: A form of divination that involves gazing into reflective surfaces like mirrors, water, or crystal balls to receive visions.

Sex Magic: The channeling of sexual energy as a force of manifestation or union with divine energies.

Shamanism: A spiritual tradition involving trance, journeying, and communication with spirits for healing and guidance.

Sigil: A stylized symbol representing a specific magical intent, often created through a process of abstraction and charged with energy.

Spiritual Baths: Ritual baths infused with herbs, salts, and prayers to cleanse energy or prepare for magic.

Spirituality: A personal and intuitive relationship with the sacred that may or may not include religion or deity worship.

Tarot: A deck of 78 symbolic cards used for spiritual guidance, reflection, and divination.

Thelema: A magical philosophy founded by Aleister Crowley, centered on the discovery and expression of one's True Will.

Tools (Ritual Tools): Physical objects used in magic to symbolize elements or channel energy—commonly include wand, athame, chalice, and pentacle.

True Will: In Thelemic philosophy, the divine purpose or deepest calling of a person's soul.

RECOMMENDED READING

Ceremonial Magic

Agrippa von Nettesheim, Heinrich Cornelius. *Three Books of Occult Philosophy*. Edited by Donald Tyson, Llewellyn Publications, 2018.
A compendium of modern ritual theory and correspondences.

Bardon, Franz. *The Key to the True Kabbalah*. 6th ed. Merkur Publishing, 2015.
Step-by-step techniques for understanding occult Kabbalah.

Crowley, Aleister. *Magick: Liber ABA, Book 4*. Edited by Hymenaeus Beta, Weiser Books, 2021.
Crowley's master text on the principles and practice of magic.

Kraig, Donald Michael. *Modern Magick: Twelve Lessons in the High Magickal Arts*. 3rd ed. Llewellyn Publications, 2010.
A structured course for learning modern ceremonial magic.

Regardie, Israel. *The Golden Dawn: The Original Account of the*

Teachings, Rites, and Ceremonies of the Hermetic Order. 7th ed. Llewellyn Publications, 2016.

Witchcraft, Wicca, and Nature Magic

Buckland, Raymond. *Buckland's Complete Book of Witchcraft*. Rev. ed. Llewellyn Publications, 2002.
    Workbook-style guide to both solitary and traditional witchcraft.

Cunningham, Scott. *Wicca: A Guide for the Solitary Practitioner*. Llewellyn Publications, 2010.
    A fantastic beginner's guide to solitary Wicca.

Farrar, Janet, and Stewart Farrar. *The Witches' Bible: The Complete Witches' Handbook*. Phoenix Publishing, 1996.
    Comprehensive Alexandrian Wicca rituals and sabbat lore.

Greer, John Michael. *The Druidry Handbook: Spiritual Practice Rooted in the Living Earth*. Weiser Books, 2006.
    Eco-centered Celtic practices that complement nature magic.

Hutton, Ronald. *The Triumph of the Moon: A History of Modern Pagan Witchcraft*. Oxford University Press, 2019.
    Scholarly history of witchcraft from its origins to modern Wicca.

Starhawk. *The Spiral Dance*. 20th Anniversary ed., HarperOne, 1999.
    Unique blend of feminist spirituality and ritual ideas for witches.

Energy Work

Avalon, Arthur, translator. *The Serpent Power: The Secrets of Tantric and Shaktic Yoga*. Dover Publications, 1974.
    Classic source on kundalini and chakra awakening.

Bruce, Robert. *Energy Work: The Secrets of Healing and Spiritual Growth.* Hampton Roads, 2007.
    Clear, hands-on exercises for raising and directing life force.

Judith, Anodea. *Wheels of Life: A User's Guide to the Chakra System.* Rev. and expanded ed., Llewellyn Publications, 2012.
    Comprehensive modern guide to the seven-chakra model.

Thich Nhat Hanh. *The Miracle of Mindfulness: An Introduction to the Practice of Meditation.* Beacon Press, 1999.
    Breath-centered meditations that builds steady inner power.

Divination

Baynes, Cary F., translator. *The I Ching or Book of Changes.* 3rd ed., Princeton University Press, 2010.
    Ancient Chinese text for strategic insight through hexagrams.

Greer, Mary K. *Tarot for Your Self: A Workbook for Personal Transformation.* 35th Anniversary ed., Weiser Books, 2019.
    Interactive workbook that strengthens tarot intuition.

Parker, Julia, and Derek Parker. *The Complete Book of Astrology.* Updated ed., DK Publishing, 2018.
    User-friendly reference for natal charts and forecasting.

Pollack, Rachel. *Seventy-Eight Degrees of Wisdom: A Tarot Journey to Self-Awareness.* Weiser Books, 2019.
    Deep symbolic exploration of the Rider-Waite-Smith deck.

Folk Traditions

Black Elk, Nicholas, and John G. Neihardt. *Black Elk Speaks: Being the Life Story of a Holy Man of the Oglala Sioux.* University of Nebraska Press, 2014.

First-hand account of Lakota visions and ceremonies.

Harner, Michael. *The Way of the Shaman: A Guide to Power and Healing*. HarperOne, 1990.
    A guide to journeying techniques in core shamanism.

Rogers, Nicholas. *Halloween: From Pagan Ritual to Party Night*. Oxford University Press, 2002.
    Explores the pagan folk customs associated with Halloween.

Mysticism & Religion

Armstrong, Karen. *A History of God: The 4,000-Year Quest of Judaism, Christianity and Islam*. Ballantine Books, 1993.
    Chronicles the rise of monotheism in three major faiths.

Bhikkhu Bodhi, translator. *The Noble Eightfold Path: Way to the End of Suffering*. Buddhist Publication Society, 2010.
    Concise guide to Buddhist ethics and meditation.

Easwaran, Eknath, translator. *The Bhagavad Gita*. Nilgiri Press, 2007.
    Key Hindu scripture on duty, devotion, and yoga.

Shah, Idries. *The Sufis*. Octagon Press, 2014.
    Stories and teachings that illuminate Islamic mysticism.

Starr, Mirabai, translator. *The Interior Castle* by Saint Teresa of Ávila, Riverhead Books, 2004.
    Christian roadmap to contemplative union with the Divine.

BIBLIOGRAPHY

Adler, Margot. *Drawing Down the Moon: Witches, Druids, Goddess-Worshippers, and Other Pagans in America Today.* Revised and expanded edition. Penguin Books. 2006.

Agrippa von Nettesheim, Heinrich Cornelius. *Three Books of Occult Philosophy.* Edited by Donald Tyson. Llewellyn Publications. 2018.

Armstrong, Karen. *A History of God: The 4,000-Year Quest of Judaism, Christianity and Islam.* Ballantine Books. 1993.

Avalon, Arthur, translator. *The Serpent Power: The Secrets of Tantric and Shaktic Yoga.* Dover Publications. 1974.

Bardon, Franz. *The Key to the True Kabbalah.* 6th edition. Merkur Publishing. 2015.

Baynes, Cary F., translator. *The I Ching or Book of Changes.* 3rd ed., Princeton University Press, 2010.

Bodhi, Bhikkhu. *The Noble Eightfold Path: Way to the End of Suffering.* Buddhist Publication Society, 2010.

Bhikkhu Ñāṇamoli and Bhikkhu Bodhi, translators. *The Middle Length Discourses of the Buddha.* Wisdom Publications. 2005.

Black Elk, Nicholas, and John G. Neihardt. *Black Elk Speaks: Being the Life Story of a Holy Man of the Oglala Sioux.* University of Nebraska Press. 2014.

Blavatsky, Helena P. *Isis Unveiled.* Quest Books. 1997.

Buckland, Raymond. *Buckland's Complete Book of Witchcraft.* Revised edition. Llewellyn Publications. 2003.

Cavendish, Richard, ed. *The Encyclopedia of the Unexplained: Magic, Occultism, and Parapsychology.* Routledge & Kegan Paul. 1974.

Crowley, Aleister. *Magick: Liber ABA, Book 4.* Edited by Hymenaeus Beta. Weiser Books. 2021.

Cunningham, Scott. *Wicca: A Guide for the Solitary Practitioner.* Llewellyn Publications. 2010.

DuQuette, Lon Milo. *The Chicken Qabalah of Rabbi Lamed Ben Clifford.* Weiser Books. 2001.

Easwaran, Eknath, translator. *The Bhagavad Gita.* Nilgiri Press. 2007.

Ellwood, Robert S., and Harry B. Partin. *Religious and Spiritual Groups in Modern America.* Routledge. 1988.

Farrar, Janet, and Stewart Farrar. *The Witches' Bible: The Complete Witches' Handbook.* Phoenix Publishing. 1996.

Greer, John Michael. *The Druidry Handbook: Spiritual Practice Rooted in the Living Earth.* Weiser Books. 2006.

Greer, Mary K. *Tarot for Your Self: A Workbook for Personal Transformation.* 35th Anniversary ed., Weiser Books, 2019.

Harner, Michael. *The Way of the Shaman: A Guide to Power and Healing.* HarperOne. 1990.

Hutton, Ronald. *The Triumph of the Moon: A History of Modern Pagan Witchcraft.* Oxford University Press. 2019.

Judith, Anodea. *Wheels of Life: A User's Guide to the Chakra System.* Revised and expanded edition. Llewellyn Publications. 2012.

Kraig, Donald Michael. *Modern Magick: Twelve Lessons in the High Magickal Arts.* 3rd ed. Llewellyn Publications, 2010.

Moss, Robert. *Conscious Dreaming: A Spiritual Path for Everyday Life.* Harmony Books. 1996.

Parker, Julia, and Derek Parker. *The Complete Book of Astrology.* Updated edition. DK Publishing. 2018.

Pinch, Geraldine. *Egyptian Mythology: A Guide to the Gods, Goddesses, and Traditions of Ancient Egypt.* Oxford University Press. 2004.

Principe, Lawrence M. *The Secrets of Alchemy.* University of Chicago Press. 2013.

Regardie, Israel. *The Golden Dawn: The Original Account of the Teachings, Rites, and Ceremonies of the Hermetic Order.* 7th ed. Llewellyn Publications, 2016.

Rogers, Nicholas. *Halloween: From Pagan Ritual to Party Night.* Oxford University Press. 2002.

Shah, Idries. *The Sufis.* Octagon Press. 2014.

Starr, Mirabai, translator. *The Interior Castle* by Saint Teresa of Ávila. Riverhead Books. 2004.

Strassman, Rick. *DMT: The Spirit Molecule.* Park Street Press. 2001.

Thich Nhat Hanh. *The Miracle of Mindfulness: An Introduction to the Practice of Meditation.* Beacon Press. 1999.

Turner, Victor. *The Ritual Process: Structure and Anti-Structure.* Aldine. 1969.

Vaughan-Lee, Llewellyn. *The Sufi Path of Love: The Spiritual Teachings of Rumi.* State University of New York Press. 1995.

www.ingramcontent.com/pod-product-compliance
Lightning Source LLC
Chambersburg PA
CBHW060152130626
46556CB00006B/2610